The Freedom of Information Act: A Catalyst for Public Governance Advancement In Nigerian Public Service Institutions

NGOZI EMMANUELA MADUKA

The Freedom of Information Act: A Catalyst for Public Governance Advancement In Nigerian Public Service Institutions

GALDA VERLAG 2018

Bibliografische Information der Deutschen Nationalbibliothek
Die Deutsche Nationalbibliothek verzeichnet diese Publikation in der Deutschen
Nationalbibliografie; detaillierte bibliografische Daten sind im Internet über
http://dnb.ddb.de abrufbar.

© 2018 Galda Verlag, Glienicke

ISBN 978-3-96203-057-5 (Print)
ISBN 978-3-96203-058-2 (E-Book)

PREFACE

The idea behind this monograph came from early childhood concerns about the state of public services in Nigeria. Over the years, the country has experienced a spate of new projects initiated by government which were eventually abandoned. These abandoned public infrastructures prompt concerns (queries/questions) such as why the funds invested in these new infrastructural projects are not directed towards maintaining already existing government infrastructures (roads, schools and hospitals); or why the appropriate government agencies do not seek the opinion of the public on these issues.

Over the years, the issue of public service reforms in Nigeria has formed the subject matter of many academic articles, conferences and roundtables and workshops. There is in existence a vast wealth of literature on public reforms thus, making it difficult to determine a suitable approach which does not focus on recommending the enactment of a new act or criticism of the existing legal framework, among others. This monograph thus aims at determining how public governance can be optimally achieved within the existing legal framework.

The ideas of this monograph took several months to materialise and get structured in a logical and scholarly manner. My gratitude goes to Mr. David Oluwagbami, a senior colleague at the Nigerian Institute of Advanced Legal Studies, for his guidance in writing this monograph.

DEDICATION

In memory of my dear friend and colleague Mr. Oyetunde Araga.

TABLE OF CONTENTS

1

INTRODUCTION

Africa since the independence years of the 1960's has suffered from socioeconomic decline,[1] significantly contributed by the lack of progressive institutional and law development policies and strategies. As Baderin observes, the modest progress made so far in the areas of law and institutional development can be used as a step stool for reaching higher socioeconomic development.[2] The first step is to identify the relevant and effective laws whose implementation will initiate and promote socioeconomic development.

Most government initiatives for socioeconomic, legal and institutional development in most African regions do not focus on the African socioeconomic and political-legal situation and its unique challenges.[3] According to the World Bank, three main factors are responsible for this. Firstly, *'lack of theory of impact of law on development, and practitioners thus had no way to prioritise reforms or predict the effects of various measures'*. Secondly, there was *'little participation by the lawyers and others in the target country who would either carry out the reforms or who would be affected by them'*. And lastly, the initiative *'focused on the formal legal system to the exclusion of customary law and other*

---

[1] Wangari Maathai, *The Challenge for Africa: A New Vision* (William Heinemann, 2009) 10

[2] Moshood A. Baderin, Law and Development in Africa: Towards a New Approach (2011) 1 NIALS *Journal of Law And Development* 1, 8

[3] Ibid. p. 8

informal ways in which many in developing nations order their lives.[4] These factors, as iterated by the World Bank, stem from the defective assumption that the enactment of a law will be an effective instrument to achieve development goals,[5] without consideration to the sociopolitical situation of that country which will affect effective direct transplantation of a law to a different system.[6]

This premise is attributable to the poor performance of most laws in Nigeria received as English law (common law, doctrines of equity, statutes of general application and statutes and subsidiary applications) by legal transplant during the British colonial system.[7] The English laws form a substantial part of Nigerian law[8] and significantly influence the Nigerian legal system. Although most the original laws containing the received English law have been amended or repealed, a significant part of the present laws reflect old or new laws enforce in Britain.

The public service laws and rules presently enforce in Nigeria are a reflection of the outdated public policy implementation and public services delivery rules which were preeminent during the nineteenth century to the late 1980s; they also centre bureaucratic systems and hegemony of professionals in the public service,[9] with little or no considerations to the public service users. Like most other laws, the public service laws and rules enacted during the colonial times,* which were by legal transplant, have been unable to address the unique challenges affecting the effective management and administration of the public service, causing it to perform poorly since Nigeria gained independence in

---

[4] World Bank Group, 'Law and Development Movement' http://siteresources.worldbank.org/INTLAWJUSTINST/Resources/LawandDevelopmentMovement.pdf accessed 4th June 2018; David M. Trubek and Alvaro Santos, 'Introduction: The Third Moment in Law and Development Theory and Emergence of a New Critical Practice' in D.M. Trubek and A. Santos (Eds.), *The New Law and Economic Development: A Critical Appraisal* (Cambridge University Press, 2006) 1–18

[5] David M. Trubek and Alvaro Santos, Introduction: The Third Moment in Law and Development Theory and Emergence of a New Critical Practice in D.M. Trubek and A. Santos (Eds.), *The New Law and Economic Development: A Critical Appraisal* (Cambridge University Press, 2006) 1–18

[6] Moshood A. Baderin, Law and Development in Africa: Towards a New Approach (2011) 1 NIALS *Journal of Law And Development* 9

[7] Lanre Fagbohun, Introduction to Law: Nigerian Legal System in Dapo F. Asaju (Ed.), *Readings in General Studies: Nigeria and African Studies* (2nd Ed., LASU Press, 2006)

[8] Obilade Olusegun, *The Nigerian Legal System* (Sweet & Maxwell, 1979) 10

[9] Hood, C., A Public Management for All Seasons? (1991) 69 *Public Administration* 3–19.

* this was the period when public service institutions were established within Nigerian

1960. The factors contributing to the recurrence of these challenges can be summarised as poor public financial management and budgeting, flawed public administrative and reporting structure[10] and unsuccessful public infrastructure and asset management policies. In a bid to address these challenges, a number of reforms were initiated by the government to improve the management and administrative structures in the public service. Some reforms were embedded in civil service rules and codes of conduct to monitor and control excesses in government administration. But this approach only achieved short-term success, as it could not address new challenges. In fact, some reforms themselves became a clog to effective public administration and management.

Unfortunately, most public service reforms failed to focus on the foundational issues which affected the effective implementation of the public service laws, which was the inability to recognise the paradigm shift of the sociopolitical atmosphere of the country after independence in 1960 from 'colonial master' to 'civil servants' governance structure. The 'colonial master' system of governance did not recognise the need for the involvement or opinion of the public in any sector of government administration, and this significantly reflected in the public service rules and laws. As Jody Freeman has noted, 'the historical inattention to this complex reality might stem in part from a tendency among administrative law scholars to eschew empiricism, or from their continuing conviction that agencies are the most important actors in the administrative arena'.[11]

Generally, laws are recognised effective instruments of economic development,[12] which are used for the effective running of institutions and attainment of developmental objectives,[13] and which evolve over time as ideas and practices change.[14] The inability of the new independent government to recognise the need to change the relevant public service laws and rules to reflect the political change from the colonial system of government where

---

[10] Ogunrotifa A. Bayo, Federal Civil Service Reform in Nigeria : The Case of Democratic Centralism (2012) 1(10) JRIERC http://www.academia.edu/2046090/FEDERAL_CIVIL_SERVICE_REFORM_IN_NIGERIA_THE_CASE_OF_DEMOCRATIC_CENTRALISM accessed 17th April 2016

[11] Jordy Freeman, The Private Role in Public Governance (2000) New York University Law Review 73 (3) 593

[12] Charles F. Sherman, Law and Development Today: The New Developmentalism (2009) German Law Journal 9 (10) 12581273

[13] T. M. Orcan, Law in Aid of Development (Ghana Publishing, 1978) 17

[14] David Trubek and Alvaros Santos n. 5 p.1

public opinions were not sought, to a system of governance where public service administrators and managements were seen as serving the people and not vice versa, created a fundamental challenge in the public service system. As Trubek and Santos rightly opined, law as an instrument of development evolves over time,[15] as such, periodic changes should be introduced into laws to reflect changes in ideas and practices,[16] if such laws must remain relevant and effective instruments of development. The failure of the new independent government after Nigeria's independence in 1960 to recognise the negative impact the colonial system of public administration had on the new democratic governance structure contributed immensely to the downward spiral of public service administration and subsequent public service reforms, as public services laws and rules became barriers to public service management and administration. In contrast, jurisdictions like Singapore retained core features from colonisation and adopted post-independence policies and models of public management to reform the civil service system. These reforms selectively introduced New Public Management policies which adopted market based principles, meritocratic principles of recruitment and promotion, a strict bureaucratic hierarchy and administrative impartiality, strong and enforceable anti–corruption measures,[17] payment of competitive market salaries,[18] and established responsive public service delivery models.[19] These reforms have progressively evolved for continuous improvement of public service to achieve sustained development in the public sector and high

---

[15] Ibid.

[16] David M. Trubeck, Law and Development in the Twenty-first Century (2009) *Law and the New Developmental State (LANDS) Research Papers*, pp 1–2 http://www.law.wisc.edu/gls/lands. html accessed 4th June 2018

[17] UNDP-GPCSE, From Old Public Administration to the New Public Service: Implications for Public Sector Reform in Developing Countries (2016) p. 6 http://www.undp.org/content/dam/undp/library/capacity–development/English/Singapore%20Centre/PS-Reform_Paper.pdf accessed 9th May 2018

[18] Jon S.T. Quah, Ensuring Good Governance in Singapore: Is This Experience Transferable to Other Asian Countries? (2013) *International Journal of Public Sector Management* 26 (5) 401–420.

[19] Eliza Wing–Yee Lee and M. Shamsul Haque, The New Public Management Reforms and Governance in Asian NICs: A Comparison of Hong Kong and Singapore (2006) *Governance* 19 (4) 605–626

scores in international governance indicators.[20]

A review of previous civil service reforms reveals the absence of the two major pillars of public governance: structural transformation in the management and administration of public organisations, and the involvement of the public (stakeholders) in public organisation reforms. These are the pillars of public governance. The former recognises the what, how and when of public needs, while the latter requires the establishment of a legitimate channel for correspondence with public stakeholders, i.e. public service users. It was perhaps in government's acknowledgment of the latter that the Executive arm of government initiated the Freedom of Information (FOI) bill that was subsequently passed by the National Assembly. The Freedom of Information Act (FOIA)[21] is a sustainable legal framework and an advancement tool for the maintenance of a legitimate channel of correspondence between stakeholders and the management of public service organisations. One objective of the FOIA is to make public records and information easily accessible to the public.[22] Access to public information is important to encourage public engagement in the management of public service organisations. The FOIA gives stakeholders the right and formal access to the official documents and records necessary to engage the management of public organisations and ensure that management observes public governance principles. However, the failure to give legitimate access for the involvement of public stakeholders in the management and administration of public service organisations in the relevant public service laws contributes significantly to the failure of public service management and administration.

Public governance as a concept stems from the principles of corporate governance. Corporate governance is more commonly applied to the private sector[23] but there is now a growing awareness of the need to introduce its core principles on administration and management in the public sector, with a view

---

[20] UNDP-GPCSE, *From Old Public Administration to the New Public Service: Implications for Public Sector Reform in Developing Countries* (2015) p. 6 http://www.undp.org/content/dam/undp/library/capacity-development/English/Singapore%20Centre/PS-Reform_Paper.pdf accessed 17th May 2018

[21] Freedom of Information Act 2011 Cap. A2 LFN 2014

[22] Ibid.; Media Rights Agenda, A Citizen's Guide to the Freedom of Information Act 2011 (Media Rights Agenda 2011) 1

[23] Martin S. Mulyadu, *The Importance of Corporate Governance in Public Sector* (2012) 1 GBERJ 25, 31

the responsibilities of the parties involved in the enforcement of public governance principles and their specific roles. The final segment concludes the paper.

2

CONCEPTUAL FRAMEWORK

Public Governance

To understand the concept of public governance, the term 'governance' must be defined. Governance is the 'coordination of institutions and agency in a given policy area towards collective objectives'.[31] Rhodes defines governance as the machinery of 'self organizing inter-organizational networks' that function both with and without government to provide public services.[32] Traditionally, the major actors in governance and policy were the government, but this mode was critiqued as inefficient, expensive and serving the interest of the public service professionals rather than the citizens.[33] This led to the emergence of New Public Governance (NPG) theory which describes the plural nature of the contemporary state and includes citizens as major actors who contribute to the governance and delivery of public services.[34] This led to the creation of the universal concept of public governance.

Public governance can be defined as a framework of accountability to taxpayers, public service users and public enterprise stakeholders within which

---

[31] Wangari Maathai, *The Challenge for Africa: A New Vision* (William Heinemann, 2009) 10

[32] Moshood A. Baderin, Law and Development in Africa: Towards a New Approach (2011) 1 NIALS *Journal of Law And Development* 1,8

[33] Helen Dickinson, *Performing Governance: Partnerships, culture and New Labour* (Macmillan, 2014)

[34] Helen Dickinson 31

government corporations, organisations and other public service providers take decisions to achieve objectives set towards the needs of public service users and the protection of the interests of public enterprise stakeholders.[35] Its objective is to maintain regulatory accountability, reporting, transparency and disclosure[36], with the focus on service users and public needs[37] in order to ensure ethical conduct in leadership (selflessness, integrity, objectivity, fairness)[38] and proper stewardship of public assets and resources.[39]

Public governance embodies different principles on accountability, improved service delivery, responsive communication, as well as leadership and ethics, among others. These principles are incorporated into the management and administration of public service organisations to ensure that excellent public governance principles are developed to establish a leadership based on a vision for strategies, objectives and accomplishments.[40] Through this, the government and its agencies carry out public services with appropriate transparency and disclosure, as their activities can be scrutinised by stakeholders. This motivates and increases public participation, ensuring that the objectives of public service organisations will deliver anticipated public services. Public governance is a useful tool to improve economic efficiency and growth, enhance investor confidence,[41] boost participation, strengthen accountability mechanisms, and open channels of communication[42] between public service organisations and their stakeholders.

---

[35] David M. Trubek and Alvaro Santos, 'Introduction: The Third Moment in Law and Development Theory and Emergence of a New Critical Practice' in D.M. Trubek and A. Santos (Eds.), *The New Law and Economic Development: A Critical Appraisal* (Cambridge University Press, 2006) 1–18

[36] Hong Kong Institute of Certified Accountants, *Corporate Governance for Public Bodies: A Basic Framework* (May, 2004) 4 http://app1.hkicpa.org.hk/publications/corporategovernanceguides/eframework_guide.pdf accessed 11th October 2016

[37] Audit Commission n35

[38] Hong Kong Institute of Certified Accountants n36 p 8

[39] Ibid. p 12

[40] Audit Commission n35

[41] OECD, *OECD Principles of Corporate Governance* (OECD Publishing, 2004) p. 11 https://www.oecd.org/corporate/ca/corporategovernanceprinciples/31557724.pdf accessed 4th Oct 2016

[42] Ayodele Adelaja Adekoya, 'Corporate Governance Reforms in Nigeria: Challenges and Suggested Solutions'(2011) 6 (1) 38 JBSGE http://www.jbsge.vu.edu.au/issues/vol06no1/Adekoya.pdf accessed 7th October 2016

According to Osborne, the five components of public governance are sociopolitical, public policy governance, administrative governance, contract governance and network governance.[43]

i. Sociopolitical governance pertains to institutional relationships within society, and challenges the supremacy of the government over other societal actors. The government relies on other societal actors for legitimacy and impact.[44]

ii. Public policy governance concerns the interactions within a multi-stakeholder policy network and how the public policy process is created, governed and directed.[45]

iii. Administrative governance is concerned with the effective application of public administration within the contemporary state.[46]

iv. Contract governance deals with the contractual relationship in the delivery pf public services, where public organisations cease to possess absolute control over the public service delivery system.[47] Rather the rights, powers and duties emanating from public service delivery are shared by multiple stakeholders.[48]

v. Network governance relates to 'self-organising inter-organisational networks'[49] which implement public policy and deliver public services and functions with or without the government to provide public services.[50]

These components make an important reference for jurisdictions which have public governance plans aimed at improving the management structure of their public service organisations. As a multi-stakeholder contractual concept, effective engagement of all internal (management and employees) and external (public service users forces) are determinant factor which ensures

---

[43] Stephen Osborne, The (New) Public Governance: a suitable case for treatment? in Stephen Osborne (ed.), *The New Public Governance? Emerging Perspectives on the Theory and Practice of Public Governance* (Routledge, 2010) 6

[44] Ibid.

[45] Ibid.

[46] Ibid.

[47] Donald Kettl, *Sharing Power: Public Governance and Private Markets* (1993, The Brookings Institution)

[48] Stephen Osborne n43 p7

[49] Rhodes n32

[50] Stephen Osborne n43 p7

that strategic plans meet the needs of public service users.[51] The practice of a multi-stakeholder contractual relationship in public service management has gained widespread acceptance in most jurisdictions; for instance, the United Kingdom (UK) has a framework for applying the principles of corporate governance[52] in the public sector that was established to engage the public with the management of public institutions in order to boost public trust and confidence in the sector.[53] Similar frameworks in Australia,[54] New Zealand[55] and Hong Kong[56] have been used to achieve significant improvement in public service management and delivery.

Public Institutions and Organisations

Public organisations and institutions share significant similarities and are sometimes considered to constitute a typology. The opposite of private institutions,[57] public institutions are non–profit, limited liability public legal entities that carry out economic and commercial activities[58] for the public good. Their aim is to serve the public's interest by performing activities that are beneficial to society.[59] They are funded by taxes, grants, special contributions, as well as income from economic activities and other sources of funding.[60]

---

[51] Aleksandras Patapas, Alvydas Raipa et al., *New Public Governance: The Track of Changes* (2014) 4 (5) IJBSR http://www.researchgate.net/publication/272625263_New_Public_Governance_ The_Tracks_of_Changes accessed 14th July 2016

[52] Audit Commission n35

[53] Audit Commission, *Trust in the Public Sector*, www.auditcommission.gov.uk accessed 17th April, 2016

[54] Australian Public Service Commission, *Building Better Governance*, http://www.apsc.gov. au/__data/assets/pdf_file/0010/7597/bettergovernance.pdf accessed 24th August, 2017 See also Australian National Audit Office, *Public Sector Governance*, https://www.anao.gov.au/sites/g/ files/net616/f/2014_ANAO%20–%20BPG%20Public%20Sector%20Governance.pdf accessed 24th August, 2017

[55] State Service Commission, *Governance of Crown Entities*, http://www.ssc.govt.nz/crown–entity–governance accessed 24th September, 2017

[56] Hong Kong Institute of Certified Public Accountants, n36

[57] http://thelawdictionary.org/public–institution/ accessed 4th July 2016

[58] Gloteka, *Establishment of a Public Institutions*, http://www.gloteka.lt/en/public_institution accessed 4th July 2016

[59] Ibid.

[60] Ibid.

Public institutions consist of different organisational forms that provide public services,[61] e.g. government ministries/agencies, nonexecutive state institutions (legislative and judiciary bodies), government bodies providing education and healthcare, as well as state–owned enterprises and corporate bodies that provide public services on behalf of the government[62] and are managed through formalised structures designed to regulate their activities and performance.[63] Public organisations can develop into institutions by attaining a specific key feature of strong effective management and administration[64] while acquiring other institutional characteristics.[65] They encompass all public bodies such as nationalist industries, public corporations, local authorities and other machinery of government that provide public services.[66] Some scholars have stressed that not all public organisations attain the status of an institution, owing to their inability to acquire key institutional characteristics. In this context, however, we consider public organisations as those government ministries or agencies that provide public services including those that have attained institutional status.

Public Service and Civil Service

'*Public service*' as a term lacks a universal definition owing to the fluidity in its interpretation for different contexts. A technical–economic meaning of the term refers to the kind of services the government commonly provides. [67]An interpretation of the term in an organisational context defines '*public service*' as a bureaucratic organisation made up of public servants who are

[61] State Service Commission, n55

[62] World Bank, *The World Bank Approach to Public Sector Management* 2011–2020:

[63] Jean–Claude Thoenig, Institutional theories and public institutions: Traditions and appropriateness in Peters Guy and Jon Pierre (eds), *Handbook of Public Administration* (SAGE, 2003) 22 https://hal.archives–ouvertes.fr/halshs–00139954/document accessed 4th July 2016

[64] Arjen Boin & Tom Christensen, The Development of Public Institutions: Reconsidering the Role of Leadership (2008) 40 *Administration & Society* 271, 275

[65] Philip Selznick, *Leadership in Administration: A Sociological Interpretation.* (University of California Press, 1984).

[66] Farnham D., Horton S., Managing Private and Public Organisations in Farnham D., Horton S. (eds.) *Managing the New Public Services.* (2nd Ed., Macmillan, 1993) 28

[67] Trine Syvertsen, The Many Uses of the "Public Service" Concept, (1999) 20 *Nordicom Review* 6 https://pdfs.semanticscholar.org/0919/8c809843e25b4850368aa9174723cbf433af.pdf accessed 26th March, 2018.

employed to implement policies, programmes, projects and services on behalf of the government.[68] The 1999 Nigerian constitution defines public service as *'the service of the Federation in any capacity in respect of the Government of the Federation'*.[69] These includes: the civil service, the armed forces and other security agencies, parastatals, public enterprises and statutory corporations, educational institutions, the arms of government (executive, legislative and judiciary) and the levels of government (federal, state and local), among others.[70] These organisations constitute the government's mechanisms for executing policies and programmes, and delivering services which adequately meet the needs of the citizenry and promote common good. The functions of the public service include designing and implementing public services, monitoring and evaluating performance of organisations (Public, Private and Non–Governmental Organisations), among others. Through these functions, public services make the state visible to its citizens, often forming the principal tangible link between governments and their people.[71] Similar to the term *'public service'*, the term *'civil service'* lacks a standard definition owing to the variations in the functionality of the term. According to s318 of the 1999 constitution, civil service means *'service of the Federation in a civil capacity as staff of the Office of the President, the Vice–President, a Ministry or department of the Government of the Federation assigned with the responsibility for any business of the Government of the Federation'*. The World Bank defines the civil service to cover government employees in central government and only in general administrative tasks.[72] The civil service is regarded as a subset of public service and a core permanent administrative arm of the government.[73] It includes government officials working in government ministries, departments and agencies, who advise, develop and implement government policies and programmes and manage day–to–day activities.[74]

---

[68] Junaidu B. Marshall & Aminu M. Murtala, Public Service In Nigeria–An Overview of Functions And Code of Conduct, *Global Journal of Politics and Law Research* (2015) 3 (1) 62

[69] *The Constitution of the Federal Republic of Nigeria* 1999 (as amended) Cap C23 LFN 2010

[70] Ibid. s169

[71] Steven Van de Walle & Zoë Scott, *The Role of Public Services in State And Nation–Building: Exploring Lessons from European History for Fragile States* (GSDRC Research Paper, 2009) http://www.gsdrc.org/docs/open/con68.pdf accessed 26th March, 2018

[72] Ann Evans, *Civil Service and Administrative Reform: Thematic Paper* (IEG Working Paper 2008) http://siteresources.worldbank.org/EXTPUBSECREF/Resources/civil_service_thematic_paper.pdf accessed 27th March, 2018

[73] Sumedh Rao n30

[74] Ibid.

According to Schiavo–Campo and Sundaram, the civil service is important for six reasons: good governance, administration of public goods and services, economic policy improvement, public revenue and expenditure management, fiscal sustainability management, and institutional development promotion.[75]

Public Governance, Corporate Governance and Good Governance

'Public Governance' and *'Corporate Governance'* are two concepts with significant characteristics, specifically on measures to improve management and administration in an organisation. Corporate governance can be defined as a set of relationships between a company's management, board, shareholders and other stakeholders[76] which provides the structures and processes through which the management of a company achieves its legitimate objectives.[77] The framework of corporate governance is provided in best–practice codes for a company's board and management in order to prevent corporate failures.[78] Public governance encompasses all that corporate governance represents to the extent of applicability. The corporate governance code provisions apply to the board and management of publicly listed companies and private companies.[79] Public governance operates through principles that guide the board and management of government–owned corporations as well as organisations and institutions that offer public service.[80] The implementation of these principles serves as a guide to promote accountability, improve public service delivery and establish communication channels with public stakeholders. *'Public governance'* is not synonymous with *'good governance'*

---

[75] Schiavo–Campo, S., & Sundaram, P, Government Employment And Compensation—Facts And Policies. In *To Serve and To Preserve: Improving Public Administration in a Competitive World.* (2001) 367–420 http://www.adb.org/sites/default/files/improving–public–administration.pdf accessed 27th March, 2018

[76] http://www.oecd.org/dataoecd accessed 10th April, 2016

[77] John Parkinson, Corporate Governance and the Regulation of Business Behaviour in Sorcha MacLeod (ed.) *Global Governance: A Quest for Justice* (Hart Publishing, 2006)

[78] SEC, *Abstract: Code of Corporate Governance* http://www.sec.gov.ng/code–of–corporate-governance-.html accessed 13th July 2016

[79] *Securities and Exchange Commission Code of Corporate Governance for Public Companies* 2011 http://www.sec.gov.ng/files/CODE%20OF%20CORPORATE%20GOVERNANCE%20FOR%20PUBLIC%20 COMPANIES.pdf accessed 10th October 2016

[80] Audit Commission n35

although the concepts are similar. In a nutshell, good governance is the *'promulgation of the normative models of social, political and administrative governance by supranational bodies such as the World Bank'.*[81] It is concerned with the exercise of fairness, justness and adherence to the rule of law, equity and fairness in the management of a country's economy[82] as well as allocation and governance of public resources.[83] One of its key principles enunciates that all key players in decision making must be recognised to ensure accountability and transparency. Public governance, on the other hand, describes principles that assist governing boards, as well as the management teams of public and public–private organisations providing public services or managing public enterprises, to establish and maintain a clear focus on objectives, performance, transparency and accountability based on the needs of public service users as well as the interests of stakeholders of public enterprises.[84] Public governance may thus be defined as a derivative of good governance.

Public Service Stakeholders

In general terms, stakeholders are identifiable persons or groups who have legitimate claims to an organisation[85] and can affect its objectives[86] or be affected by its goals.[87] The classification of stakeholders differs in the private and public sectors. The former identifies primary and secondary stakeholders.[88] The stakeholders of the latter are generally categorised as government departments, politicians, lobby groups, staff, the community/

---

[81] Rhodes Williams n32

[82] IFAD, *Good Governance: An Overview* (September, 1999) http://www.ifad.org/gbdocs/ eb/67/e/EB–99–67–INF–4.pdf accessed 11th October 2016

[83] Chris Cornforth, *The Governance of Public and Non-Profit Organisations. What Do Boards Do?* (2003, Routledge)

[84] Hong Kong Institute of Certified Accountants, n36

[85] Charles W. Hill and Thomas M. Jones, Stakeholder–Agency Theory (1992) 29(2) 133 *Journal of Management Studies* http://onlinelibrary.wiley.com/doi/10.1111/j.1467–6486.1992.tb00657.x/ pdf accessed 14th July,2016

[86] Edward R. Freeman and David L. Reed, Stockholders and Stakeholders: A New Perspective on Corporate Governance (1983) 25 *California Management Review* 88

[87] Joseph Weiss, *Business Ethics: A Stakeholder's Approach & Issues Management Approach* (5th edn, South Western 2009) 43

[88] Clarkson Max, A Stakeholder Framework for Analyzing and Evaluating Corporate Social Performance (1995) 20 *Academy of Management Review* 92–117

citizens, partners and alliances, unions, customers, and public service users, among others.[89] In this context however, only users of public services are described as stakeholders.

---

[89] Sandra Beach, Kerry Brown, Robyn Keast, *Together Now: Stakeholders in Government Agencies* (International Research Society for Public Management Conference, Brisbane, 2008)

3
THEORETICAL FRAMEWORK

The concept of public governance is deeply rooted in various theories of traditional and contemporary public administration as well as those of public and management reform. Contemporary reform theories deviate from the traditional or bureaucratic approach that centred on hierarchy, rules, permanence and stability in the civil service,[90] although the traditional approach was no doubt successful in its day.[91] Osborne suggests that the evolution of public policy implementation and public services delivery may be classified in a tripartite regime model: public administration (PA), new public management (NPM) and new public governance (NPG).

Public Administration (PA) was dominant from the late nineteenth century through the late 1970s/early 1980s.[92] According to Hood, the key elements that characterised PA were dominance of rule of law, focus on set rules and guidelines, bureaucratic implementation of policies, politics of administration within the public organisations, incremental budgeting and supremacy of professionals in public service delivery.[93] Following the inability of PA to

---

[90] Ali Farazmand, Global Administrative Reforms and Transformation of Governance and Public Administration in Ali Farazmand & Jack Pinkowski (eds.) *Handbook of Globalization, Governance, and Public Administration* (1st edn. Routledge, 2006) 351

[91] Ibid.

[92] Stephen Osborne, The (New) Public Governance: a suitable case for treatment? in Stephen Osborne (ed.) *The New Public Governance? Emerging Perspectives on the Theory and Practice of Public Governance* (Routledge, 2010) 1

[93] Christopher Hood, Public Management for All Seasons? (1991) 69 *Public Administration* 3–19."

effectively meet all the social and economic needs of the citizenry during the British welfare state of 'cradle to grave',[94] PA was heavily criticised by academics and elites as ineffective to the practice of public policy implementation and public service delivery.[95] This led to the emergence of NPM.

The NPM theory argues for discarding the bureaucratic model of PA where emphasis is laid on implementing the decisions of political masters, a situation which puts the civil service under their political control.[96] It focuses on the need for public organisations to run like private businesses, as it focuses on improving efficiency in input and output while ensuring improved customer service and cost reduction.[97] This largely protects the civil service from the unstable effects of government politics and its uncertainties. The management teams of public organisations would be independent and focused on strategies for effective and efficient public service centred on public values and needs.

NPM is regarded as a gold standard for public management reform;[98] it is not regarded as a blueprint, but it provides a source where new ideas and values on public management can be selectively applied to improve management practices for specific public organisations.[99] This is based on the idea that the administrative capacity of government organisations would be more effective and efficient if their organisational processes and structures are managed at private-sector standards.[100] The NPM theory challenges the traditional or bureaucratic model of public administration,[101] focusing on private sector management techniques, entrepreneurial leadership, input and output control, performance management and audit, and disaggregation of public services to their most basic units emphasis on their cost management.[102] This led to the evolution of management as a legitimate role in public service organisations.

[94] Stephen Osborne n92 p.3

[95] Rhodes Williams n32

[96] Ali Farazmand n90 p.893

[97] Ibid.

[98] Ibid.

[99] Ari Salminen, New Public Management and Finnish Public Sector' in Alberto Amaral, V. Lynn Meek (eds.) *The Higher Education Managerial Revolution?* (Kluwer Academic Publishers, 2003) p. 89

[100] Ali Farazmand n90

[101] Aidan Rose, *Results-Orientated Budget Practice in OECD Countries* (2003 Overseas Development Institute Working Paper) 209 https://www.odi.org/sites/odi.org.uk/files/odi-assets/publications-opinion-files/2035.pdf accessed 24th August 2017

[102] Stephen Osborne n 92 p.4

The nexus between NPM and public governance is identifiable in its focus on private sector managerialism and performance management. Managerialism is the transfer of private–sector managerial practices and skills to the public sector on the premise that the apparent success of the private sector is largely attributed to the management practices and skills adopted there.[103] This adoption would bring about the much needed boost in the public sector by significantly improving efficiency and output through a dynamic management structure that responds more effectively to the ever changing public service needs while representing public values. Lähdesmäki[104] has presented the four principle "E's" of NPM: economy, efficiency, effectiveness and ethics in administration of the public sector.

Despite the success of NPM in western countries like the Anglo-American, Australian, and Scandinavian regions, this theory is considered restrictive in some developing economies as a result of its limited applicability to the existing governance mechanism.[105] Some sub-Saharan African countries face challenges with the implementation of NPM in their civil service structure and process owing to lack of infrastructure, political will and a sense of ownership, as well as having a weak capacity, among other factors.[106] This invariably makes PA dominant in public policy implementation and public services delivery in these regions.[107] NPM has been criticised further as being a sub-school of PA which is lacking in theoretical base,[108] as well as its focus on '*intraorganisation*' which is a misfit in a plural world and inapplicability

---

[103] Michael Pidd, *Measuring the Performance of Public Services: Principles and Practice* (Cambridge University Press, 2012) p. 11

[104] Lähdesmäki, K., New Public Management and Reforming Public-sector Management: A Study of the Principles of Organisational Efficiency, Economy and Effectiveness, and Public Sector Entrepreneurship, Performance Management, and their Accountability in *Public Sector Management Reforms in Finland from the late 1980 to the Early 1990s* (University of Vasa, 2003) 113

[105] Gelas Rubakula, The New Public Management and its Challenges in Africa (2014) 4 (4) *JJSTE* 86

[106] Ibid.

[107] Kickert, W, Public Governance in the Netherlands: An Alternative to Anglo-American 'Managerialism, (1997) 75 (4) *Public Administration* 731–752.

[108] George Frederickson and Kevin Smith, *The Public Administration Primer* (Westview Press, 2003)

of its private sector technique[109] as a result of its geographical variegation.[110] Of particular interest is the criticism owing to its contradictory emphasis. For instance, NPM emphasizes centralization and decentralization of policy, budgeting, standard and strategy.

The limitations of NPM and changing times create new public service administration challenges and demand a new approach to public administration reform. The solution to this was to make government more *'businesslike'* in some areas of the public sector to *'hollow out'* the government and make the sector more efficient.[111] This resulted in the fragmentation of the public sector through contracts with commercial and community organisations, thus leading to significant autonomy from the state.[112] As Bevir and Rhodes have noted:

> *Fragmentation created new networks but also ... incorporating both the private and voluntary sectors ... government swapped direct for indirect control, so that central departments are no longer either necessarily or invariably the fulcrum of a network. The government can set the limits to network actions: after all, it still funds the services. But it has also increased its dependence on multifarious networks.*

According to Osborne, the shift towards a networked form of governance between the government, commercial as well as community organisations described as new public governance theory.[113] NPG is considered the third tier design of public policy implementation and public service delivery, and its model is based on institutional and network theories.[114] Osborne posits both a plural and pluralist state, where the policy making system is informed from

---

[109] Les Metcalfe and Sue Richards Improving Public Management (Sage, 1991)

[110] Sandford Borins, New Public Management, North American Style, in Kathleen McLaughlin, Stephen Osborne and Ewan Ferlie (eds.) *The New Public Management: Current Trends and Future Prospects,* (Routledge,2000)

[111] Guy Peters, Managing the Hollow State in K. A. Eliassen and J. Kooiman (eds.) *Managing Public Organizations: Lessons from contemporary European Experience* (Sage, 1993)

[112] Rhodes Williams n32

[113] Stephen Osborne, The New Public Governance? (2006) 8(3) *Public Management Review* 377–87 https://www.tandfonline.com/doi/abs/10.1080/14719030600853022 accessed 2nd February 2018

[114] Stephen Osborne, The (New) Public Governance: A Suitable Case for Treatment? in Stephen Osborne (ed.) *The New Public Governance? Emerging Perspectives on the Theory and Practice of Public Governance* (Routledge, 2010) 1

multiple inter-dependent actors (public service organisations, private sector, non-governmental sector, and public service users)[115] which contribute to the delivery of public service, and where the policymaking system is informed through multiple processes respectively.[116]

NPG is conceptualized as fresh public management reform lacking a clear-cut paradigm of reference;[117] owing to the distinct elements and differing emphasis and needs of public management in each jurisdiction, this allows for fluidity as a result of its wider application. Principally, NPG's core and universal value places citizens and not the government at the centre frame,[118] thus emphasizing the public interest in making citizens co-producers of policies and the delivery of services.[119] Osborne posits that NPG theory is not a new paradigm to supersede PA and NPM; rather it is a conceptual tool which aids in the understanding of the complexities of the challenges faced by public managers.[120]

In NPG, it is imperative that ideas and interactions from multiple interdependent actors be conceptualised into questions, as this is significant for effective public policy implementation in a plural and pluralist state, rather than being; a particular focus on what public service organisations must do differently. These questions generally relate to the fundamentals of NPG; such as policy implementation, organisational and staff performance, partnership, accountability, productivity and organisational sustainability, among others.[121] This gives NPG a different starting point which presents enduring inter-organizational relationships of trust, relational capital and relational contracts, which are regarded as core governance mechanisms.[122]

---

[115] Stephen Osborne, Zoe Radnor and G. Nasi, A New Theory for Public Service Management? Towards a (Public) Service Dominant Approach. *The American Review of Public Administration* (2013) 43 (2) 135–158.

[116] Stephen Osborne n92 p.384

[117] Mark Robinson, *From Old Public Administration to the New Public Service: Implications for Public Sector Reform in Developing Countries* (UNDP-Global Centre for Public Service Excellence, 2015) 9 http://www.undp.org/content/dam/undp/library/capacity-development/ English/Singapore%20Centre/PS-Reform_Paper.pdf accessed 9th of March, 2018

[118] Joycelyn Bourgon, Responsive, Responsible and Respected Government: Towards a New Public Administration Theory. *International Review of Administrative Sciences*, (2007) 73 (1) 7

[119] Mark Robinson n118 p9

[120] Stephen Osborne n92 p6

[121] Ibid.

[122] Tony Bovaird, Developing New Forms of Partnership with the 'Market' in the Procurement of Public Services, *Public Administration* (2006) 84, 1

Owing to NPG's focus on multi-interdependent actors for governance processes, service effectiveness and outcomes for public service delivery and policy implementation, the decision-making process is riven with power inequalities which must be navigated to successfully ensure progression.[123] To address power inequalities and divergences in intra-organisational interactions, a partnership model which harmonises multiple views should be established to aid effective policy implementation. Also, public managers need to *acquire skills that go beyond capacity for controlling or steering society in pursuit of policy solutions to focus more on brokering, negotiating and resolving complex problems in partnership with citizens*.[124] Implementation of the NPG approach in public service management demands an *open and accessible, accountable and responsive government, beyond the formal approaches of public administrators* response to citizens' complaints. Borugon's proposed four elements for new public administration best describes the role the government and public service administrators should adopt for efficient implementation of the NPG approach:[125]

1. building collaborative relationships with citizens and groups of citizens;
2. encouraging shared responsibilities;
3. disseminating information to elevate public discourse and to foster a shared understanding of public issues;
4. seeking opportunities to involve citizens in government activities.

---

[123] Stephen Osborne n92 p6

[124] Mark Robinson n118 p10

[125] Joycelyn Bourgon, n119

4
REFORMS IN THE NIGERIAN CIVIL SERVICE SYSTEM

The origin, structure and performance of the Nigerian civil service can be traced to the British colonial era.[127] It was established as a vehicle for development and public service delivery.[128] The public administration system in force in the United Kingdom was adopted for the Nigerian civil service. This system focused on a traditional system exactly as the PA system, where a neutral competent civil servant works within a structure of hierarchical authority.[129] The 'traditional' system measure for performance in the civil service focused on legal and accounting grounds, rather than on the basis of the actual performance of tasks and the outcomes for citizens.[130] The principles of the traditional system were based on 'standardized establishment procedures', which means the public sector was governed through a formalized system for recruitment, pay, grading, and other aspects of internal management.[131] The concept of accountability flowed

---

[127] Nwanolue, B. and Victor Iwuoha, The Nigerian Civil Service And Promotion of Sustainable Human Development: A Critical Analysis (2012)1 (9) *Arabian Journal of Business and Management Review* p.12

[128] Murana Asimiyu Olalekan, Salahu Moshood Olayinka, and Ibrahim Basirat Omotayo, The Impacts of The Nigerian Civil Service Reforms on Effective Service Delivery (2016) VII *International Journal of Politics and Good Governance*

[129] Guy Peters, The Changing Nature of Public Administration: From Easy Answers to Hard Questions (2003) 5 *Viešoji Politika Ir Administravimas* 8

[130] Ibid. p.9

* This was discussed in detail in the earlier part of this work at page

[131] Ibid.

upwards as civil service officials answered to their political masters and the government provided same benefit to all citizens. This was the conception of fairness, which in practice produced inequities as public service needs differed in different regions.[132]

This traditional system of civil service administration that was practised during the colonial period by the British government in Nigeria was known as the pre-reform era in the United Kingdom.[133] After independence in 1960, the administrative leadership of the civil service that took over from the colonial masters continued with the traditional system of civil service administration without consideration to the challenges this system posed on effective civil service administration. The failure to restructure the system to suit the developmental needs of the public,[134] heralding the deep decay in the civil service system was the failure to restructure the system to suit the developmental needs of the public. Ironically, during the post-colonial era, specifically during the late 1970s, the traditional system or PA system of civil service administration had come under criticism by academics and political elites,[135] and was on a 'terminal decline' in the United Kingdom.[136] The criticisms were mainly based on the principles of PA* and the challenges they posed to efficient civil service administration. This paved the way for the reform and rise of the NPM system of civil service administration.

Unfortunately, the post-colonial civil service leadership relied heavily on the civil service blueprint of the colonial masters which was predominately based on archaic and defective PA system. Their inability to identify the defects of the PA system led to indiscipline and inability to achieve set goals, thus worsening the condition of the system.[137] The volatile political climate in the country during the late 19060s and 1970s (shortly after independence) significantly contributed to civil service administration challenges.[138] In a bid to address these challenges, the civil service underwent various structural and attitudinal reforms as compelled by frequent civilian and military regime

---

[132] Ibid.

[133] Ibid.

[134] Murana Asimiyu Olalekan, n128 p.3

[135] Ramesh Mischra, The Welfare State in Crisis, (1984, Wheatsheaf)

[136] Chandler J. Public Administration: A Discipline in Decline, (1991) 9 *Teaching Public Administration*, 39–45.

[137] Murana Asimiyu Olalekan, n128

[138] Michael M. Ogbeidi, Political Leadership and Corruption in Nigeria Since 1960: A Socio-economic Analysis (2012) 1 (2) *Journal of Nigerian Studies* 6

changes.[139] Oddly, neither the government nor the civil service administrators considered the prospects of the newly adopted NPM system in the British civil service.

Since 1963, several civil service reforms have been undertaken in the Nigerian civil service, namely, the Morgan Salary and Wage Commission (1963), the Adebo Commission (1971), the Udoji Public Service Review Commission (1974), the Dotun Philips Civil Service Reform Commission (1988), the Allison Ayida Civil Service Reform (1995), the Pension Reform (post-1999), the Reform on Restructuring and Repositioning of Ministries which established the Bureau of Public Service Reforms (2004), the Monetisation Policy (2003), Reform for Down-Sizing in the Public Sector (2014), Financial Regulations and Anti-Corruption Policy, the Service Delivery Reform Initiative which established SERVICOM (2004), the Steve Oronsaye Committee (2007), the Adamu Fika Committee (2013), and the Treasury Single Account (TSA) system (2016).[140]

The most recent and significant reforms are the post-1999 civil service reforms after Nigeria's transition from a military system of government to a democratic system of government. The first major reform in 1999 was the change in the structure of the government which focused on improving the economy through the restructuring and resuscitation of specific government ministries.[141] This reform was significant owing to the need for government and the public service to reflect the new system of government in place. Subsequently numerous civil service reforms have been initiated, such as: The Integrated Payroll and Personnel Information System (2007) which reduced the cost of governance and improved the quality of government payroll administration; Pension Reforms (2004) which introduced the contributory pension scheme; Public Procurement Reforms (2003) which established the Budget Monitoring and Price Intelligence Unit (BMPIU); Public Enterprise Reforms which privatised some unproductive and inefficient public enterprises; Pay Reform (2007) which led to the consolidation of salaries, the minimum wage and pay increase for public servants; Monetisation Policy reform which provided government with more transparency in the management of salaries and fringe benefits by curbing excesses; National Statistical System Reform

---

[139] Iyayi, S.A., The Civil Service Reforms in Nigeria since Independence in Bello-Imam (ed.), *50 Years of the Nigerian Project: Challenges and Prospects* (College Press 2010) 247

[140] Constitution of the Federal Republic of Nigeria n69 s 80 (1)

[141] BPSR, *Public Service Reforms in Nigeria 1999–2014 A Comprehensive Review* (2015)

(2004) which led to the transformation of National Bureau of Statistics (NBS) into a competent and professional organisation; Tenure Policy Reform (2009) which introduced the Tenure Policy through which permanent secretaries would hold office for 4 years, renewable for another 4 years and no more, subject to satisfactory performance; Transparency and Accountability Initiatives and reforms (2011) which improved transparency and accountability in governance; Anti-Corruption reforms (2004) which established anti-corruption agencies to tackle corruption and improve transparency in public service; Health Insurance reform which established the National Health Insurance Scheme (2005) which has made it possible for public servants to get insurance for affordable health care services; Justice System Reforms (2011) which increased scrutiny on the behaviour of judges and on cases of possible misconduct by judges; Postal Service (NIPOST) Reforms which improved the quality of postal service by reviving a comatose service to the public, improvement of process efficiency, operational efficiency, customer focus, and cost control among others; SERVICOM reform (2012) which improved service delivery and established complaints mechanisms and compliance evaluation in all MDAs; Performance Management Reforms which harmonised the performance management system and developed Key Performance Indicators (KPIs) and Ministerial Scorecards; Reform of the Office of the Head of the Civil Service of the Federation (OHCSF) which is the highest hierarchy of civil service leadership, this reform restructured and streamlined the OHCSF for greater effectiveness and devised strategies for reduction in operational costs and devolution of 34 functions to MDAs; Reform of the Federal Civil Service Commission (FCSC) recaptured the core principles and values for which each Commission was set up and addressed credibility problems and inefficiency challenges; Electoral Reform which increased the level of independence of the Independent National Electoral Commission (INEC) in operational and financial terms; Information Sector Reforms which implemented strategies for public information management in collaboration with sector partners to improve public awareness and understanding of government programmes; Public Financial Management Reforms which adopted and implemented International Public Sector Accounting Standard and reduced bureaucracy, red tape and the delays in processing and payments of government bills; among others.

These civil service reforms focused on improving civil servants' welfare, curbing of sharp practices, mismanagement and diversion of public funds, as well as combat lack of probity and accountability,[142] which were rife during the military era.[143] These reforms, though relevant for each period, rather considered shallow issues and none dealt with the fundamental issue of identifying the nexus between citizens' participation in public service management and improved public service delivery; a public governance centred reform. These reforms failed to transform the Nigerian system from the archaic and bureaucratic PA approach of public service administration which was in force during the colonial administration into dynamic citizen-centred reforms such as the NPM or NPG approach. Since the late 1970s this has been a core consideration in most developed economies with an efficient public service delivery system.[144]

The two reforms which initiated a form of citizen-centred strategy are the SERVICOM and Performance Management reforms. The SERVICOM reform established a form of responsive communication with the citizens by creating a platform for the public to make complaints about the quality and promptness of public service delivery in most civil service offices.[145] However, this did not incorporate the public governance principles of citizens' participation on how public service delivery can be improved. The Performance Management Reforms which identifies key performance indicators which is the basis for evaluating and determining the performance of federal civil service organisations unfortunately did not perform optimally. Unfortunately, the performance management reforms, which were meant to identify key performance indicators and to be the basis for evaluating and determining the performance of federal civil service organizations, did not perform optimally; human constraints that limited the Annual Performance Evaluation Report (APER) process; challenges with linking performance to pay and promotion, inability to develop and implement institutional, departmental, and individual performance measures for each civil service organisation; the inability of replacing examinations with outcomes of appraisals or developing and adopting new criteria which factor outcome of appraisals in the promotion of employees, inability to resolve the issue of promotion in PMS pilot MDAs when promotion examinations are still in use in non-pilot MDAs, the difficulty

---

[142] Rosemary Anozode, Joseph Okoye and Emma Chukwuemeka, Civil Service Reforms in Nigeria: The Journey So Far in Service Delivery, (2013) 3 (1) *American Journal of Social And Management Sciences* 19

[143] Ibid. p.21

[144] See the earlier reference of the British civil service reform

[145] SERVICOM, *The SERVICOM Book* (SERVICOM, 2006)

of applying Public Service Rules in the PMS pilot MDAs, and the challenge of ensuring that all issues relating to the professionalization of Human Resources (HR) are fully resolved.[146]

Also, the emergence of democracy in May 1999, after long years military rule, created new challenges. One of such challenges was the creation of new public institutions to serve both public service needs and compensate political god-fathers.[147] Consequently, this resulted in a bloated workforce that encouraged inefficiency, laziness, ineptitude, corruption and waste of government revenue through recurring expenditure to sustain the new public institutions.[148] Owing to the wielding of political influence in the appointment of top civil service officials and nepotism in general civil service employment,[149] work efficiency and productivity plunged as public service was mainly a means to serve the interests of bureaucrats.

Consequently, the oversight of a citizens' based reform that creates a legitimate nexus between the citizens and the management of public service organisations remains a significant gap in achieving desired outcomes in public service delivery. Thus, the Nigerian public service system remains weak, inefficient and appears incapable of reforming itself.[150] Every developed economy with an efficient public service system recognises the importance of this. For instance, the Australian perspective on public service reform specifically addresses the need for improved public service delivery that centres on customer service, public involvement with policy development and an open consultation approach,[151] which are hallmarks of public governance. The United Kingdom approach to public service reforms acknowledges the essentiality of public service users' input to improve the efficiency and effectiveness of public services through advertisements and consultations.[152]

---

[146] BPSR, n141

[147] Ibid. p.21

[148] Cornelius Ofobuisi Okorie and Odo Stella, A Survey of Public Service Reforms in Nigeria: 1999 2013 (2014) 4 (10) *International Journal of Humanities and Social Science*, 269

[149] Ibid.

[150] Jacob Olufemi, and Kehinde David, Public Sector Reform in Africa: Issues, Lessons and Future Directions, (2010) 12 *Journal of Sustainable Development in Africa* 145–157

[151] Australian Public Services Commission, *The Australian Experience of Public Sector Reform*, (2015) http://unpan1.un.org/intradoc/groups/public/documents/apcity/unpan021316.pdf accessed 4th April 2017

[152] Cabinet Office, *The UK Government's Approach to Public Service Reforms* (2006) http://webarchive.nationalarchives.gov.uk/20070701080507/cabinetoffice.gov.uk/strategy/downloads/work_areas/public_service_reform/sj_pamphlet.pdf accessed 4th April 2017

Public sector management is multifaceted, as it expands beyond the traditional role of managing performance in public organisations. Several World Bank reports capture the intricate and complex linkage between a country's economic development and public sector management which is assessed through public sector performance (PSP). Public governance remains a core element in PSP is vital for the development of a sustainable and optimal public service delivery system which is significant for the development of the economy. According to the OECD, PSP is a key factor in measuring a government's performance.[153] Ideally, taxes are converted into revenues for the provision of public services and infrastructures as an indicator of a responsive and efficient government.[154] According to Raj Kumar, PSP is a standard determinant of competitiveness and it is 'essential to encourage both sound FDI and domestic private investment',[155] which are key drivers in globalisation and economic development in developing economies. This depicts the chaineffect of PSP in fostering economic development and the need for the government to put in specific measures which are essential for nurturing and sustaining FDI and domestic private investment.

Within the sub-Saharan African (SSA) region, poor performance of public institutions and the inefficacy of public sector management are associated with deteriorating economic growth which also, affects private sector performance and functioning.[156] Institutions and governance are cornerstones that attract FDI inflows as vehicles towards economic growth poverty and alleviation in the host country.[157] Public sector management plays a significant role in achieving the dividends of FDI and is required to enforce complementarity

---

[153] OECD, *Measuring and Improving Government Performance* http://www.oecd.org/site/worldforum06/38756317.pdf 19th March, 2018

[154] Konstantinos Angelopoulos, Apostolis Philippopoulos & Efthymios Tsionas, Does Public Sector Efficiency Matter? Revisiting the Relation Between Fiscal Size and Economic Growth in a World Sample (2008) https://www.gla.ac.uk/media/media_43670_en.pdf accessed 19th March, 2018

[155] Raj Kumar, Changing Role of the Public Sector in the Promotion of Foreign Direct Investment *Asia Pacific Development Journal* (2003) 10 (2) 16

[156] Nhema, Alfred, Public Administration and the Development of Africa: A Critical Assessment *Journal of Public Administration and Governance* (2016) 6 (1) 6

[157] Elizabeth Asiedu, Foreign Direct Investment in Africa: The Role of Natural Resources, Market Size, Government Policy, Institutions and Political Instability *The World Economy* (2006) 29, 63–77.

between domestic and foreign investment to enhance productivity.[158]

A general comparison of jurisdictions with efficient and strong public service management and those with poor and inefficient public service management system, indicates the linkage between PSP and economic development. According to the 2016 World Bank CPIA Africa Report, '*established*' and '*improved*'[159] countries are economically resilient and have better policy and institutional quality, while countries with '*slipping*' economies[160] have weakened policy and institutional quality.[161] Thus, it is not unforeseen that the Nigerian economy remains stunted and is grabbling with a slipping economy.

Public sector management is also an effective instrument for achieving nation building. Steven Van de Walle and Zoë Scott[162] elaborated on Rokkan's summary[163] succinct summary on how public services can be used to achieve nation building through the processes of penetration, standardisation and accommodation. Although their case study focused on Western Europe, this validates their argument as it can be seen within this region that public service is used to achieve nation building. The process of penetration aims to establish the penetration of the state and public services is an important instrument to achieve this. Through the establishment of infrastructures for public services, deconcentrated government administration offices are set up which strengthen the presence and control of the government at the rural, urban and remote areas. The process of standardisation creates a common culture expressed through the creation of similar public services and administrative procedures for all citizens in different regions. This extends to public service employees who need to identify with the wider apparatus by connecting with other public service employees. The final process discusses accommodation, which

---

[158] Bilali Jumanne and Choong Keong, Foreign Direct Investment and Public Sector Management and Institutions: The Acquaintances in sub-Saharan Africa (SSA) Low-Income Economies *African Journal of Economic Review* (2017) V (II)

[159] These include: Cote D'Ivoire, Senegal, Mali, Kenya, Ethiopia, Tanzania, and Rwanda.

[160] These include: Zambia, Malawi, Botswana, Nigeria, South Africa, and Chad

[161] World Bank Group, *CPIA Africa: Assessing Africa's Policies and Institutions* (2017) http://documents.worldbank.org/curated/en/891501500349324004/pdf/117514-REVISED-96p-WB-CPIA-Report-July2017-ENG-v16.pdf accessed 21st March, 2018

[162] Steven Van de Walle and Zoë Scott, *The Role of Public Services in State and Nation-Building: Exploring Lessons from European History for Fragile States* (GSDRC Research Paper, 2009) www.gsdrc.org/docs/open/con68.pdf accessed 3rd April 2019.

[163] Stein Rokkan, Dimensions of State Formation and Nation-Building: A Possible Paradigm for Research on Variations within Europe, in C. Tilly, (ed.), *The Formation of National States in Western Europe.*(Princeton University Press, 1975) 562

acts as a counterbalance to penetration and standardisation. Public services are used by the politicians for political power brokering and accommodation to maintain a delicate balance between political groups in post-conflict countries.[164] Through processes of accommodation, competing centres of power within the state are safeguarded against, by using public services as a means to buy loyalty and discourage disloyalty. This is an effective means of pacification in divided societies where quotas are used in the distribution of public offices.[165] Promises of public service facilities and jobs are used by political lords as excellent instruments to seal political deals.

Unfortunately, one of the major challenges in public sector management in Nigeria is the overuse of the process of accommodation at the expense of the processes of penetration and standardisation. As a nation riddled with ethnic and religious conflicts, civil war and a quota system in the distribution and appointment in public offices, public services are predominately used as a political instrument to reward loyalty to political lords. Likewise, political lords shut down or frustrate certain public service organisations in a bid to punish disloyalty or intimidate political rivals. Inadvertently, the Nigerian constitution encourages the overuse of the process of accommodation by welding so much power to appoint top civil service officers on the executive arm of government who are purely elected into office based on majority votes. Both the federal and state executive arms of government hold the power to appoint top staff in the civil service. At the federal level, the President has power by virtue of sections 170 & 171 of the constitution to appoint persons to hold or act in the offices of Secretary to the Government of the Federation; Head of the Civil Service of the Federation; Permanent Secretary in any Ministry or Head of any Extra-Ministerial Department of the Government of the Federation. In exercising this power, section 171(5) requires the President to have regard to the federal character of Nigeria and the need to promote national unity and section 172 requires the appointees to observe and conform to the Code of Conduct. Similarly, at the state level, the Governor of each state has power, by virtue of sections 207 and 208 of the constitution, to appoint persons to hold or act in the offices of Secretary to the Government of the State; Head of the Civil Service of the State; Permanent Secretary or other chief executive in any Ministry or Department of the Government of the State howsoever designated. In exercising this power, section 208 (4) requires the

---

[164] Richard Stillman, *Public Administration: Concepts and Cases* (7th ed. Houghton Mifflin Company, 2000) 18

[165] Yusuf Bangura, *Ethnic Inequalities and Public Sector Governance* (2006, Palgrave) 77

governor to '*have regard to the diversity of the people within the state and the need to promote national unity*' and appointed persons are required to '*observe and conform to the Code of Conduct*'.[166]

By virtue of this, the executives at the federal and state levels are given power to appoint without a corresponding duty to ensure the exercise of such powers are exercised in a fiduciary capacity on behalf of the citizens who are directly impacted by such appointments. Furthermore, in the absence of adequate '*checks and balances*' to monitor the exercise of this power, a system of '*winner takes all*' is established which promotes tyranny of the executives by allowing the furtherance of interests of the supporters of the government to secure their position and weaken their opponents. This presupposes the use of civil service appointments an instrument to award loyalty and discourage disloyalty. As in most post-crisis third world countries, the predominant use of public services in Nigeria as an instrument for rewarding loyalty and discouraging disloyalty fosters deep decay in the public service system and encourages neglect in public service management. The power and ability of political lords to hire and fire at will creates a milieu which allows corruption, nepotism and favouritism to thrive at the expense of optimal public service administration and management. Since appointment or employment to (especially top or managerial positions) the public sector is not categorically based on qualification or achievements in service, the mechanism or need to measure performance and encourage hard work becomes unnecessary.

Owing to the pitfalls of the '*winner takes all system*', the United States of America's jurisdiction has put effective '*checks and balances*' in place to ensure elected officials do not use the influence of their office to secure positions at the expense of good governance. This is made possible by the propriety rights known as the '*Due Process Clause*' given to federal civil service employees by Congress to protect them against politically motivated terminations except on grounds of just cause and written charges as stated in the Lloyd-LaFollette Act.[167] This repudiates any act by the executive to use the public jobs (which is regarded as private property)[168] as political property. In the United Kingdom, the civil service system is very similar to that of Nigeria, and the reason is not far-fetched: the Nigerian civil service system was inherited from the British colonial government. The civil service is protected from being used

---

[166] Constitution of the Federal Republic of Nigeria n69 s209

[167] Executive Order 101 (July 27, 1897). See also http://www.pogoarchives.org/m/cots/Lloyd-LaFollette-Act.pdf accessed 10th April, 2018

[168] Charles A. Reich, The New Property, *The Yale Law Journal*, (1964) 73 (5)

for political advantage for the party in power. The Cabinet Secretary[169] is the highest ranking civil servant, appointed by the Prime Minister. Though the Cabinet Secretary is appointed by the Prime Minister, the position is estopped from being used as a political instrument to carry out the interest of the party at the expense of the general public. The checks and balances put in place by virtue of the criterion for appointment of the Cabinet Secretary are based mainly on ability to execute set responsibilities to foster efficiency and growth in the civil service. The power of the Prime Minister to appoint a Cabinet Secretary of choice is mainly to aid collective decision making with the party's agendas or policies. Furthermore, the Chief Executive Officer of the Civil Service (CEO CS) who is appointed by the Prime Minister with the job specification of ensuring the civil service (Whitehall), works more efficiently through better deals for taxpayers from commercial decisions, easy digital transition of the civil service, ensuring the best people with the right skills are in the civil service, and major projects are managed better.[170] In essence, the role of the CEO CS is to ensure reforms which will improve service and efficiency of the civil service is achieved.

Thus though the appointment of the heads of civil service lies with the Prime Minister, the well retrenched system of convention and a powerful civil service structure where the Prime Minister is held to account for incompetence ensures public interest is protected and preserved.[171] In addition, the Citizen's Charter programme ensures that the service users are empowered to ensure set standards of public service are met, and that any failure entitles the service user to compensation. These measures are put in place to secure the independence of the civil service from being used as an instrument for rewarding loyalty by elected executives; it also aims to ensure the public service preserves its key role as an instrument of nation building and economic development for the benefit of every citizen as a core value of public governance. One major achievement of a public governance centred reform is the promotion of accountability and transparency through an inclusive governance structure which allows citizens' participation and

---

[169] This position was split into three posts: Cabinet Secretary, Head of the Home Civil Service and Cabinet Office Permanent Secretary in 2011

[170] https://www.gov.uk/government/news/chief-executive-for-civil-service-appointed accessed 10th April 2018

[171] Don Russell, *The Role of the Executive Government in Australia* (Papers on Parliament No. 41, 2003) https://www.aph.gov.au/~/~/link.aspx?id=0C347E23897C4885BB8B5E5875D21141&_z=z accessed 10th April 2018

involvement in public service management. Through this, citizens are allowed access to government information which is vital to monitoring and promoting accountability and transparency in public institutions. This disrupts the trends of using the civil service as political instruments of loyalty or exclusive process of accommodation and creates a conducive setting which enables public service institutions to achieve their key roles in the society, through incentivising performance where recruitment and promotion are merit based, pay and bonuses are performance based, effective performance monitoring mechanism are put in place, sustainable ethical codes are observed[172] and accountability is enforced without undue interference from political lords. Public governance recognises that public service institutions are critical for the improvement of the public's well-being. These institutions underpin all development sectors relevant for quality health, education, environmental protection, safety, and economic policies, among others;[173] as such s, must be grounded in transparency, innovations and citizens' participation to increase trust between the citizens and the government.[174] This makes the state tangible to the citizens and invariably creates a sense of loyalty and belonging to the state;[175] it also ensures the public gets fair returns on their taxes.

---

[172] Bunse, Simone and Fritz, Verena, *Making Public Sector Reforms Work: Political and Economic Contexts, Incentives, and Strategies*, (Policy Research Working Paper 6174, World Bank 2012); See also Garcia-Sanchez, I., Rodriguez-Dominguez, L., and Gallego-Alvarez, I., Effectiveness of Ethics Codes in the Public Sphere: Are They Useful in Controlling Corruption? *International Journal of Public Administration*, 34, 190–95

[173] World Bank Group n161

[174] IDA, *Towards 2030: Investing in Growth, Resilience and Opportunity* (World Bank, 2017) http://documents.worldbank.org/curated/en/471761467993490105/IDA18-IDA18-overarching-theme-towards-2030-investing-in-growth-resilience-and-opportunity accessed 22nd March 2018

[175] Eugen Weber, *Peasants Into Frenchmen: The Modernization of Rural France* 1870–1914. Stanford (Stanford University Press, 1976)

5

PUBLIC GOVERNANCE APPLICABILITY AND ENFORCEMENT

The principles of public governance are benchmarked on the three fundamental principles of corporate governance openness: integrity and accountability.[176] These principles are adapted to reflect the key characteristics of public sector entities owing to the more complex range of political, economic and social constraints and influences which public sector management is faced with. Thus, the application of these principles are not as clear-cut in public organisations as it in private organisations; as such, each jurisdiction designs a system by which the management of public organisations adopts and implements these principles in the public sector. In most jurisdictions, these principles are legitimately incorporated into the rules, codes of conduct, policies and regulations of most public service organisations,[177] and are applied by the management of public organisations to boost accountability, as well as to promote effective leadership and public trust. They also encourage clarity in policies, strategies and objectives, thus reflecting the views and needs of public service users.[178] For instance, in the United Kingdom, the Nolan Report adopted seven 'principles of public life', (selflessness; integrity; objectivity; accountability; openness; honesty; and leadership) reflecting public governance principles

---

[176] Cadbury Committee (U.K.), *Report of the Committee on the Financial Aspects of Corporate Governance,* (1992) http://cadbury.cjbs.archios.info/report 22nd March, 2018

[177] Government of Western Australia PSC, *Public Sector Governance* https://publicsector.wa.gov.au/public-administration/public-sector-governance 28th August, 2017

[178] Audit Commission n35

which must be incorporated into the codes of conduct of public entities and terms of responsibilities for holders of public office.[179]

In Nigeria, the rules and laws governing public service institutions include the public service rules,[180] scheme of service,[181] conditions of service,[182] establishment act[183] and code of conduct.[184] Public governance principles are not clearly expressed in these rules, but there are, there are subtle reflections of public governance principles in the code of conduct. Predominately, the public service rules and establishment acts make administrative provisions for issues pertaining to appointments and leaving the service, discipline, emoluments and increments, annual performance evaluation reports (APER) and certificate of service, examinations in law and official publications, medical and dental procedures, compensation, insurance and personal effects, petitions and appeals, leave, free transport facilities within Nigeria, courses of instruction within and outside Nigeria, allowances, petitions and award committee, reward or outstanding service, and application of public service rules to federal government parastatals. The conditions of service simply make human resource policies relating to appointment of service, eligibility for appointment, employee records, vacancies, probation and confirmations, transfer, secondment, termination, resignation, retirement, pension, discipline, salaries, performance management, administrative duties of staff among others, specifically for each public service organisation. The scheme of service list the different cadres in each public service organisation. Conversely, the Code of Conduct provisions as contained in the fifth schedule of the Nigerian constitution reflect the public governance principle of integrity for public office-holders by prohibiting acts which may taint their

---

[179] IFAC, *Governance in the Public Sector: A Governing Body Perspective International Public Sector Study* (2001) 11 http://www1.worldbank.org/publicsector/pe/befa05/Study_13_ Governance.pdf accessed 22nd March, 2018; See also Richard Jarvis, *The UK Experience of Public Administration Reform "Current Good Practices and New Developments in Public Service Management"* (Common Wealth Secretariat, 2002)

[180] http://www.fedcivilservice.gov.ng/?page_id=284 accessed 16th April, 2018

[181] http://www.ohcsf.gov.ng/index.php/scheme-of-service accessed 18th April, 2018

[182] Each public service organisation designs its own conditions of service based on specific criterion. For example the Nigerian Institute of Advanced Legal Studies designed its conditions of service as http://nials.edu.ng/ accessed 18th April, 2018

[183] Every Nigerian government institution, agency or organization has an Establishment Act which states the duties, powers and administrative rules they must abide by.

[184] http://lawnigeria.com/LawsoftheFederation/CODE-OF-CONDUCT-BUREAU-AND-TRIBUNAL-ACT. html accessed 18th April, 2018

integrity and ethical conducts. Although the code of conduct applies to all public office-holders including elected members of the executive arm of government, selected provisions apply to civil service employees (Head of the Civil Service, Permanent Secretaries, Directors-Generals and all other persons in the civil service of the Federation or of the State). Part 1 of the Code of Conduct for Public Officers[185] prohibits civil service employees from conflict of interest,[186] receiving emoluments from different public offices,[187] operating foreign bank accounts,[188] accepting more than one remuneration position from the government after retirement,[189] accepting benefits for acts done or omitted to be done while in office,[190] accepting loans except form the government or financial institutions,[191] accepting bribes or inducement,[192] abusing official powers,[193] and falsifying information on assets declaration.[194] Assessing the rules which govern civil service employees and administration in Nigeria reveals how inept the rules are in achieving public governance. The core elements of both corporate governance and public governance are absent in the civil service rules and codes of conduct. This lacuna stalls or hinders reforms and creates no foundation for public governance to be adapted into the civil service system. According to the UNDP, public sector reforms in developing countries need to embrace a public management model that are appropriate for the jurisdiction's attributes and limitations, thus putting the interest of the citizens at the centre of the reform consistent with the new public service approach.[195] In adopting a public governance model for the Nigerian civil service reform, a vital tool which empowers the citizens and creates a legitimate platform for citizens to access relevant information from

---

[185] *Constitution of the Federal Republic of Nigeria*, Fifth Schedule, n69

[186] Ibid.

[187] Ibid. s2

[188] Ibid. s3

[189] Ibid. s4

[190] Ibid. s6

[191] Ibid. s7

[192] Ibid. s8

[193] Ibid. s9

[194] Ibid. s11

[195] GCPSE, *From Old Public Administration to the New Public Service: Implications for Public Sector Reform in Developing Countries* (2015) http://www.undp.org/content/dam/undp/library/capacity-development/English/Singapore%20Centre/PS-Reform_Paper.pdf accessed 26th March, 2018

the management of public service organisations must be utilised. Legitimate access empowers the citizens with the right to request relevant information which is necessary to monitor and evaluate the practices of the management of public service organisations. Public access to government information is a key element for building a relationship between the citizens and the government —this lays the foundation of trust.

Freedom of Information Act

The Freedom of Information Act is a vital tool for upholding trust between the citizens and the government. Trust is core in every relationship between citizens and government, most especially in relation to services which affect life, liberty, health, policing, social services and education.[196] Even if formal service and outcome targets are met, a failure of trust will effectively destroy public value.[197]

Before the enactment of the FOI Act in Nigeria, there was no form of trust between the citizens and the government, most activities of the government and its agencies were shrouded in secrecy. This created a disconnect as the citizens were ignorant of the activities of the government and such public service needs and expectations were not met; in addition, the veil of secrecy allowed for corruption fester. This led to public agitation on the need to know how the government controls and manages the affairs of state in order to make the government transparent and accountable in its administration, to monitor and curb abuse and corruption in public offices. This agitation by the public was for the enactment of a legislation that would enable them access government information easily, a transition from the Leviathan system where citizens had no right or need to ask for government information.[198]

---

[196] Audit Commission, *Creating Public Value: An Analytical Framework for Public Service Reform* (Strategy Unit, Cabinet Office, November 2002) http://archive.audit-commission.gov. uk/auditcommission/subwebs/publications/studies/studyPDF/3126.pdf accessed 9th October 2017

[197] Ibid.

[198] Patrick Birkinshaw, *Freedom of Information* (4th edn, Cambridge Press 2010) 23

The enactment of the Freedom of Information Act of 2011[199] repealed various legislations such as the Official Secret Act[200], the Evidence Act[201], the Public Complaints Commission Act[202], the Statistics Act[203], the Criminal Code[204] and other related laws which made it difficult for government institutions, organisations or employees to release government information to the public and also stopped the public from requesting information from government organisations.

The objective of the FOI Act is succinctly stated as follows:

'An Act to make public records and information freely available, provide public access to public records and information, protect public records and information to the extent consistent with public interest ...and establish procedures for the achievement of the purpose...'[205]

By virtue of the FOI Act every citizen has the right to request government information and seek access to public records and information[206] from both federal and state public institutions;[207] in addition, public records must be protected in a manner that isconsistent with the interest of the public.[208]

This right extends to public stakeholders and gives them legitimate access to request for vital information necessary to monitor and evaluate the activities of any specific public service institutions. The Act gives stakeholders the right to request for government information,[209] upon failure of the public organisation to make specific information publicly available.[210] When requesting information, *'an applicant under this Act needs not demonstrate*

---

[199] Freedom of Information Act n2

[200] Official Secret Act 1962 Cap 03 LFN 2004

[201] Evidence Act 2004 Cap 112 LFN 2004

[202] Public Complaints Commission Act 2004 Cap P37 LFN 2004

[203] Statistics Act 2007 Cap 446 LFN 2010

[204] Criminal Code Act 2004 Cap C38 LFN 2004

[205] The Preamble Freedom of Information Act 2011 n21

[206] Ibid. s1&2

[207] Ibid. s31

[208] Ayodele Afolayan, *A Critical Analysis of the Freedom of Information Act in Nigeria* (2012) https://odinakadotnet.wordpress.com/2012/08/01/a-critical-analysis-of-freedom-of-informati on-act-in-nigeria-2/ accessed 13th July 2016

[209] Freedom of Information Act 2011 n21 s1(1)

[210] Ibid. s2(2)

any specific interest in the information being applied for.[211] This means that the applicant need not justify an information request application even if demanded by the public institution. By virtue of section 2 of the FOIA public institutions are mandated to proactively publish the following information:

(1) A public institution shall cause to be published in accordance with subsection (4) of this section, the following information:

(a) a description of the organization and responsibilities of the institution including details of the programmes and functions of each division, branch and department of the institution;

(b) a list of all—

(i) Classes of records under the control of the institution in sufficient detail to facilitate the exercise of the right to information under this Act, and

(ii) Manuals used by employees of the institution in administering or carrying out any of the programmes or activities of the institution;

(c) a description of documents containing final opinions including concurring and dissenting opinions as well as orders made in the adjudication of cases;

(i) Substantive rules of the institution

(ii) Statements and interpretations of policy which have been adopted by the institution;

(iii) Final planning policies, recommendations, and decisions;

(iv) Factual reports, inspection reports, and studies whether prepared by or for the institution;

(v) Information relating to the receipt or expenditure of public or other funds of the institution;

(vi) the names, salaries, titles and dates of employment of all employees and officers of the institution;

(vii) The right of the state, public institutions, or of any private person(s)

(viii) The name of every official and the final records of voting in

---

[211] Ibid. s1(2)

all proceedings of the institution;

(e) a list of—

    (i) Files containing applications for any contract, permit, grants, licenses or agreements,

    (ii) Reports, documents, studies, or publications prepared by independent contractors for the institution, and

    (iii) Materials containing information relating to any grant or contract made by or between the institution and another public institution or private organization;

(f) The title and address of the appropriate officer of the institution to whom an application for information under this Act shall be sent, provided that the failure of any public institution to publish any information under this subsection shall not prejudicially affect the public's right of access to information in the custody of such public institution.

    (3) A public institution shall cause to be published ... the following information: a description of the organization and responsibilities of the institution including details of the programmes and functions of each division, branch and department of the institution.

        (b) A public institution shall cause to be published ... manuals used by employees of the institution in administering or carrying out any of the programmes or activities of the institution.

The information provided in section 2 are relevant to stakeholders as they encompass all necessary information necessary to monitor the duties of the employees of the public service institutions, as well as contracts or activities which involves the provision of public service(s). Stakeholders who are unsatisfied with the public service output can identify the specific division or department of the institution saddled with the responsibility of ensuring the delivery or maintenance of a specific public service. The popular phrase 'government has no face' will no longer apply as it is now possible to identify which government institution has the duty to carry out specific public services. Stakeholders are empowered with the right to request information pertaining to the activities of public service institutions to the extent the such activities affect their interests.

On the issue of promoting financial transparency to curb misappropriation and mismanagement of funds, section 2 (3) (c) (v) provides that 'A public *institution shall cause to be published ... information relating to the receipt or expenditure of public or other funds of the institution'*, thus making transparency in financial reporting easier. This provision is an effective tool that can be used to curb misappropriation or embezzlement of public funds. Although this provision does not require public institutions to make comprehensive financial reporting in a proactive manner, it should significantly promote a transparency culture in financial reporting. Stakeholders can monitor how and where public funds are spent, in order to ensure funds budgeted for the maintenance or creation of public service infrastructures are used for that particular purpose. This alerts the managers of public institutions to the fact that stakeholders can at will request to know how public funds are being spent.

Pertaining to the issue of sub-standard or poor quality infrastructure which is a major challenge in Nigeria, Section 2 (3) (e) (iii) provides that '*A public institution shall cause to be published ... materials containing information relating to any grant or contract made by or between the institution and another public institution or private organization'*. Thus, stakeholders can legitimately investigate the official contract document in the custody of the public institution to determine if the quality of infrastructure delivered is in fact as specified in the contract document. Furthermore, in cases where a public service is sourced to a private organisation, investigations may also be carried out to determine if contracts are awarded to ghost companies which are actually an avenue for '*legally*' diverting public funds into private pockets. This section can therefore help to curb the challenge of outright embezzlement of funds awarded for specific contracts and monitor the quality and duration of contract work approved for execution, thus challenging any irregularities if need be.

In essence, the right given to the public by the FOI Act to request for information from government institutions, provides legitimate solutions to address most challenges which cripple public service delivery by giving them the right to investigate, challenge and monitor compliance in the management of public service institutions, notwithstanding its complex bureaucratic administrative structure. Unfortunately, stakeholders are unwilling to engage public service institutions as a result of challenges with the enforcement of the FOI Act which impede information request applications and access to relevant government information. These challenges range from handling of information request applications,[212] interpretation challenges owing to

---

[212] Right2Info, *Nigeria: The Limits to the Freedom of Information Act* (2011) http://www.right2info.org/recent/nigeria-the-limits-of-freedom-of-information-act accessed 13th July 2015

ambiguities in specific sections of the FOIA,[213] enforcement challenges due to erroneous court interpretation of the FOI Act,[214] general unwillingness to accept the FOI request based on arguments on its applicability at the State level,[215] and practical challenges resulting from an inefficient information management system in public institutions, among others.

Furthermore, the exemption provisions of the Act which list a number of grounds for denying information requests, however lack of understanding of specific sections of the FOIA as it relates to exemptions significantly impede public access to government information as information officers[216] shy away from releasing such information applications.[217] The reason for this may be attributable to the old culture of official secrecy, as public officers hesitate to release government information for fear of facing disciplinary actions. Concerning exemption provisions, it is pertinent to note that the FOI Act allows for exempted information to be released, Although it must pass through the public interest test.

Public Interest Test[218]

The public interest test provisions are a core feature in the FOI Act which sets legal limits to protect some government information from the public[219] in order to minimise or avoid substantial harm to the government or its

---

[213] Freedom of Information Act n21 s14 (1) (b) & s 2 (3) (d) (vi); See also *Uzeogwu F.O.C vs CBN & the Attorney General of the Federation* FHC/ABJ./CS/1016/2011 and *Legal Defence & Assistant Project Ltd Vs Clerk of the National Assembly of Nigeria* FHC/ABJ/CS/336/2013

[214] *Paradigm Initiative Nigeria v Dr. Reuben Abati* Suit No FHC/ABJ/CS/402/2013 In this case the judge asserted that an information applicants must demonstrate specific interest in the information requested for. This is in clear contradiction to section 1(2) of the FOI Act

[215] *CLO v Enugu Health Commissioner* FHC/EN/M/263/2011, *Ogunlola v Oyo State House of Assembly* (M/332/12) Unreported

[216] These are employee of public institutions with the responsibility of handling information request applications.

[217] These are the sections that provide grounds for information request refusal : Freedom of Information Act s.11 (1) defence and international affairs of Nigeria; s.12 (1) law enforcement proceedings; S.14 personal information; s12 (3) commission of offence; s16 professional privilege; s17 research material prepared by a faculty; s19 (1) (b) to the extent disclosure of building plan would compromise security

[218] Ibid. s11, s12, s14,s15 and s19

[219] Paul Finn, *Official information: Integrity in Government* (Canberra , 1991) p.4

agents. The public interest test analysis is a scale for determining whether exempted information should be disclosed. Under the FOI Act, the test to be applied provides that '*an application for information shall not be denied where the public interest in disclosing the information outweighs whatever injury the disclosure would cause*.'[220] Applying the public interest test requires balancing competing interests—the public interest to know and justification for maintaining the exemption. By implication, the release of exempted information will most likely be injurious to the government or its agents; however, an in-depth analysis must be carried out to ascertain the extent of such injury. Analysing and determining the extent of injury which the release of exempted information may cause is more easily ascertainable, but the main challenge lies with the determination of what factors are relevant for consideration when defining and determining the public interest in particular cases.[221] The first onus on the decision to determine what qualifies as public interest lies with the public institution[222] and the internal review committee.[223] The second and final onus rests on the Judiciary.[224]

Public interest can generally be viewed as referring to '*public good*', which is distinct from '*what is of interest to the public*' or the '*private interests of the requester*';[225] it does not mean "that which gratifies curiosity or merely provides entertainment or amusement".[226] Thus for the public institution to determine what qualifies as public interest for each case , it is necessary to evaluate those aspects that are competing and of comparative significance in order to

---

[220] Freedom of Information Act 2011 n 21 s 11, 12, 14

[221] Ashley Savage, Leaks, *Whistleblowing and the Public Interest: The Law of Unauthorised Disclosures* (Edward Elgar Publishing Ltd, 2016) 40-64

[222] Freedom of Information Act UK 2000 s7 & s 17 http://www.legislation.gov.uk/ukpga/2000/36/contents accessed 7th September 2017

[223] Federal Ministry of Justice, *Guidelines on the Implementation of the Freedom of Information Act 2011*, (FMJ, 2013) 16, See also ICO Guidance, *Freedom of Information: Good Practice Guidance No.5* (2007) https://www.whatdotheyknow.com/request/119280/response/304644/attach/3/ICO%20Guidance%20Internal%20Review%20Time%20Limits.pdf accessed 7th September 2017

[224] Freedom of Information Act n21 s20

[225] University of York, *Public Interest Test Method Statement* https://www.york.ac.uk/records-management/foi/foi-policy/public-interest-test-method-statement/ accessed 30th August, 2017

[226] *Per Lord Campbell LJ in R v Inhabitants of the County of Bedfordshire* (1855) 24 L.J.Q.B. 81 at 84

determine what qualifies as public interest in each case.[227] In determining this, the following factors may be considered: public debate of current issues relating to the information, promotion of accountability on public expenditure, need for the public to understand and challenge government decisions, information affecting public safety,[228] and information that will ensure the government acts within its lawful authority.[229] Other considerations include the likelihood and severity of any prejudice, the age of the information, how far the requested information will help public understanding, and whether similar information is already in the public domain.[230] However, it should be made clear that '*public interest*' is not a fixed concept and the balance of public interest may change over time. It may shift as information becomes older or in the light of issues or circumstances at the time the request is being considered.[231] According to the Australian Information Commissioner Guideline[232] and the New South Wales Freedom of Information Act,[233] the factors which are irrelevant when determining the public interest, they include: the possibility of an applicant misinterpreting or misunderstanding the information, information that would cause embarrassment and loss of confidence to the government[234] and information that is highly technical etc.[235]

Under the FOI Act, exempted provisions are categorised as qualified since as the public interest test must be applied. Public institutions are mandated by both the FOIA and the courts to identify the factors that were considered in weighing the public interest against an exemption provision in order to prove whether an exemption outweighed or did not outweigh the public interest. Against this backdrop, public institutions through its Information Officers

[227] *Per Tamberlin J. in McKinnon v Secretary Department of Treasury* [2005] FCAFC 142 http://www.austlii.edu.au/au/cases/cth/FCAFC/2005/142.html accessed 30th August 2017

[228] JISC Legal Information Services & Dundas & Wilson, *Freedom of Information and the Public Interest Test* (2004) http://www.humanrightsinitiative.org/programs/ai/rti/implementation/applying_law/public_interest_uk_jisc.pdf accessed 30th September 2017

[229] *Re Heaney v The Public Service Board* (1984) 6 ALD 310 at p.323

[230] University of York, n225

[231] Ibid.

[232] Australian Information Commissioner, *FOI Guidelines* https://www.oaic.gov.au/freedom-of-information/foi-guidelines/ accessed 27th September, 2017

[233] New South Wales Freedom of Information (Amendment) Act 1992 s 59 https://www.legislation.nsw.gov.au/acts/1992-38.pdf accessed 1st September, 2017

[234] Northern Territory Information Act 2002 s50 & New South Wales Freedom of Information Act (n36) s59A Commonwealth of Australia v John Fairfax and Sons Limited (1981) 55 ALJR 45

[235] *Coulthart v Princess Alexandra Hospital and Health Service District* (2001) 6 QAR 94

and Internal Review Committee, must rigorously evaluate all relevant factors concerning that particular case in addition to considering the objective of the FOI Act before issuing a refusal notice. As stated by Mason CJ, '...*the expression 'in the public interest', when used in a statute, classically imports a discretionary value judgment to be made by reference to undefined factual matters, confined only 'in so far as the subject matter and the scope and purpose of the statutory enactments may enable.'*[236] Thus, though this allows for the use of discretion in evaluating each particular case, information officers must ensure they consider all issues relevant for each case and they must exercise this discretion in a manner consistent with the objective of the FOI Act which is to make information accessible to the public.

The issues for consideration may fall outside the ambit of FOI Act provisions and may inadvertently affect other laws pertaining to right to privacy, among others, the breach of which may be actionable. In particular section 16 provides that '*a public institution may deny an application for information that is subject to the following privileges—legal practitioner-client privilege; health workers-client privilege; journalism confidentiality privilege; any other professional privileges confidently by an Act'*. Nonetheless, according to section 27 of the FOI Act, such information may still be released if such information was released in good faith. Section 27 expressly provides:

(1) Notwithstanding anything contained in the Criminal Code, Penal Code, the Official Secrets Act, or any other enactment, no civil or criminal proceedings shall lie against an officer of any public institution, or against any person acting on behalf of a public institution, and no proceedings shall lie against such persons thereof, for the disclosure in good faith of any information, or any part thereof pursuant to this Act, for any consequences that flow from that disclosure, or for the failure to give any notice required under this Act, if care is taken to give the required notice.

(2) Nothing contained in the Criminal Code or Official Secrets Act shall prejudicially affect any public officer who, without authorization, discloses to any person, information which he reasonably believes to show

(b) mismanagement, gross waste of funds, fraud, and abuse of authority; or

(c) a substantial and specific danger to public health or safety notwithstanding that such information was not disclosed pursuant to

---

[236] *Per Mason CJ in O'Sullivan v Farrer* (1989) 168 CLR 210 at 216

the provision of this Act.

(4) No civil or criminal proceeding shall lie against any person receiving the information or further disclosing it.

Similarly in the United Kingdom, government information can be released even though it may breach provisions of others laws, such as the right to privacy and publication of personal information which are actionable under the privacy tort[237] and breach of confidentiality.[238] In *Campbell v MGN*[239] Ltd the court held that a right of privacy can only be invaded if the publication is of legitimate public concern and a defence of fair comment would also succeed if it is proved that the matter is of public interest and based on true facts even though protected by privilege.[240] This principle was applied by the court in the case of *Cook v Telegraph Media Group Ltd*:[241] that although a publication contravened Section 40 of the FOI Act (UK) and can actually damage the reputation of some members of Parliament, it was in public interest for such information to be published.

In a nutshell, section 27 provides an absolute legal protection from legal action for both information officers and stakeholders who receive exempted information without authorisation, despite its contravention of other laws. This encourages whistle-blowing to curb corruption and mismanagement of funds in public service institutions. However, a significant lapse in the FOI Act is the non-provision for confidential communication access for both public officials and the public. The significance of confidential communication access for both information officers and stakeholders is critical if the aim is to advance access to information and curb corruption. Having an established communication channel is the foundation for stakeholders to exercise their role in public governance, and failure to establish anonymous communication channels is detrimental to the advancement of public governance in Nigeria. Nigeria as a State has its unique challenges, one of which is *'guaranteed safety'*. Lack of safety for both citizens and public officers is a major reason for the lack of public stakeholders' participation. The inability of stakeholders to express their opinions, concerns and complaints without fear can be attributed to the general *laissez-faire* attitude towards the public service. A notable example

---

[237] William Prosser, Privacy (1960) 48 *California Law Review* 392-396

[238] Freedom of Information Act 2000 n222 s 41

[239] [2004]All ER 67

[240] *Waterson v Lloyd* [2011] EWHC 3197

[241] [2011] EWHC 1519

of the importance of confidential communication access is the tremendous achievements of the anonymous whistle-blowing policy initiated by the Federal Government of Nigeria to aid the Economic and Financial Crimes Commission (EFCC) in its fight against corruption.[242]

Public sector stakeholders must be properly informed on the significance of the public interest test in all exemption provisions in the Act. If an information request is denied and the reasons contained in the refusal notice are unsatisfactory, the stakeholder can, firstly, apply for a review of the refusal to the internal review committee within the public service institution. If the stakeholder is still unsatisfied with their response, an application can be made to the court. The courts' considerations when reviewing a public institution's refusal notice[243] must: examine the information requested,[244] ascertain the intent of the legislature in applicable FOI provisions,[245] analyse the public institution's discretionary value judgement with caution,[246] and identify relevant factors, principles and circumstances that the courts believe to be important to the subject matter of that particular case. The courts also specially consider the objective of the FOI Act, which is to give citizens access to information that will assist them in exercising their rights to participate in and influence issues of concern to them.[247] The court can then exercise the power to review whether the information application denial if unjustified, an order for disclosure will be made against the public institution[248] which may include a fine of N500,000.00 in favour of the applicant.[249]

The applicability of the FOI Act provisions exclusively covers public institutions,[250] private organisations that utilize public funds to perform

---

[242] Federal Ministry of Finance, *FMF—Whistle Blowing Frequently Asked Questions (FAQs)* , (2017) https://whistle.finance.gov.ng/_catalogs/masterpage/MOFWhistle/assets/FMF%20WHISTLEB LOWING%20FREQUENTLY%20ASKED%20QUESTIONS.pdf accessed 18th April 2017

[243] Freedom of Information Act n21 s19

[244] Ibid. s 22

[245] *Per Bello Aliyu in Uzoegwu v The Central Bank of Nigeria & Attorney General of the Federation* FHC/ABJ/CS/1016/2011

[246] Freedom of Information Act n21 s23, this is done in camera or ex parte to avoid the disclosure of the information

[247] Per Queensland Information Commissioner in Re Eccleston and Department of Family Services (n21) http://www.austlii.edu.au/au/cases/qld/QICmr/1993/2.html accessed 5th September 2017

[248] Freedom of Information Act n21 s25

[249] Ibid. s7(5)

[250] Ibid. s30(3)

public functions[251] and government information.[252] Private companies play a significant role in public service delivery which operates through contracts, franchises, grants, concessions, and public-private partnerships (PPP) with specific government agencies.[253] These alternative options for public service delivery have their potential strengths and weaknesses globally.[254] In Nigeria, alternative options for public service delivery have increased public service delivery in areas where the government has limited or no presence as a result of manpower and resource constraints. This to a certain degree has led to improved efficiency and productivity. A survey in Abuja[255] suggests that private companies which provide public services in the health, sanitation and electricity sectors on behalf of the government are preferable to that of government agencies.[256] Also, public services which require expertise beyond the capabilities of the government and its agencies are outsourced to private companies with requisite expertise and ability to deliver such public services.

Each of the thirty-six (36) states in Nigeria and the Federal Capital Territory in Nigeria has a public procurement agency with similar laws and a general mandate to set standards, regulate and oversee public procurement within the state. In Rivers State, for instance,[257] the Rivers State Bureau on Public Procurement (RBoPP) oversees the procurement process to ensure fairness, transparency, compliance and due process while auditing and supervising the implementation of appropriate procurement policies, among other functions[258] amongst other functions.[259] The fundamental principles for procurement are contained in Part III of the Rivers State Public Procurement Law,[260] which sets out the process for handling public procurement when a request is

---

[251] Ibid. s2(7)

[252] Ibid. s29(9)

[253] Hatry Harry, *A Review of Private Approaches for Delivery of Public Services* (Urban Institute Press, 1983)

[254] Harry Kitchen, Delivering Local/Municipal Services in Anwar Shah (eds.) *Public Service Delivery* (World Bank, 2005.) 128 http://siteresources.worldbank.org/PSGLP/Resources/Pub licServiceDelivery.pdf accessed 26th April 2018"

[255] This is the Federal Capital Territory of Nigeria

[256] Nazifi Abdullahi Darma & Muhammad Ali, An Assessment of Public Sector Service Delivery in Nigeria: A Case Study of Federal Capital Territory Area Councils, 2007–2011 (2014) 3(8) *International Journal of Development and Sustainability*

[257] This is one of the thirty six states in Nigeria.

[258] https://rsbopp.rv.gov.ng/index.php/legislations/law accessed 22nd May 2018

[259] https://rsbopp.rv.gov.ng/index.php/about-us/mandate accessed 22nd May 2018

[260] https://rsbopp.rv.gov.ng/index.php/legislations/law accessed 22nd May 2018

received from a procuring entity such as a government ministry, department or agency (MDA) within the state. The core issues for evaluation by the RBoPPA are documentations received from bidders as proof of qualification under the law to apply as a bidder;[261] in addition solicitation documents of bidders must be verified to ensure the bidder possesses relevant professional, technical, financial, infrastructural and personnel capabilities requisite for the contract.[262] A bidder will be excluded from bidding if there is evidence that:[263]

i. any supplier, contractor or consultant has… offered or given employment or any other benefit, … to a current or former employee of a procuring entity or the Bureau, in an attempt to influence any action, or decision making of any procurement activity;

ii. a supplier, contractor or consultant during the last three years prior to the commencement of the procurement proceedings in issue, failed to perform or to provide due care in performance of any public procurement;

iii. the bidder is in receivership or is the subject of any type of insolvency proceedings or if being a private company under the Companies and Allied Matters Law, is controlled by a person or persons who are subject to any bankruptcy proceedings…

iv. the bidder is in arrears regarding payment of due taxes, charges, pensions or social insurance contribution, unless such bidders have obtained a lawful permit with respect to allowances, defence of such outstanding payments or payment thereof in installments;

v. the bidder has been validly sentenced for a crime committed in connection with a project the bidder has in its management or is in any portion owned by any person that has been validly sentenced for a crime committed in connection with a procurement proceeding, or other crime committed to gain financial profit; and

vi. The bidder fails to submit a statement regarding its dominating or subsidiary relationship with respect to other parties to the proceedings and persons acting on behalf of the procuring entity participating in same proceeding or who remains in subordinate relationship with other participants to the proceedings.

---

[261] River State Public Procurement law 2008 s 14(7)

[262] Ibid. s 14(6)

[263] Ibid. s 14(8)

All procurement of goods and services on behalf of the government must be conducted by an open competitive bidding,[264] to ensure fairness, transparency and discourage undue advantage for all bidders. The evaluation, examination and acceptance of bids are to determine eligibility and to select the lowest evaluation responsive bid from bidders.[265] The successful bid is commonly selected from the lowest responsive bid, Although, the selected bidder need not be the lowest cost bidder, provided the procuring entity can show good grounds derived from the provisions of this Law.[266]

Under the Rivers State procurement law, a procuring entity or MDA may directly procure goods or services in event of an emergency or where:[267]

i.   goods, works or services are only available from a particular supplier of contractor, or if a particular supplier or contractor has exclusive rights in respect of the goods, works or services;

ii. there is an urgent need for the goods, works or services and engaging in tender proceedings or any other method of procurement is impractical due to unforeseeable circumstances giving rise to the urgency;

iii. owing to a catastrophic event, there is an urgent need for the goods, works or services, making it impractical to use other methods of procurement;

iv. a procuring entity which has procured goods, equipment, technology or services from a supplier or contractor when it determines that: (i) additional supplies need to be procured from that supplier or contractor because of standardization; (ii) there is a need for compatibility with existing goods, equipment etc.;

Although laws and regulatory measures have been put in place by both the state and federal public procurement agencies to curb corruption by prescribing punishment for specific offences which range from collusion, fraud, bid rigging, and fake documentation among others, these corrupt practices persist. There is the public perception that some private companies are avenues for government officials to collude and conspire with management to defraud the government.[268] One of the factors responsible for this is the inadequate

---

[264] Ibid. Part V

[265] Ibid. Part V

[266] Ibid. Part VI

[267] Ibid. Part VI

[268] Dare E. Arowolo & Christopher S. Ologunowa, Privatisation in Nigeria: A Critical Analysis of the Virtues and Vices (2012) 1(3) *International Journal of Development and Sustainability* 8

legal framework and weak enforcement mechanism which are unable to curb diversion of public funds through public procurement.[269] The Economic and Financial Crimes Commission (EFCC), a commission mandated to handle financial and economic crimes in the public and private sectors,[270] reports that it handles a large number of procurement-related cases. Similarly, the Independent Corrupt Practices Commission (ICPC) a commission mandated to prohibit and prescribe punishment for corrupt practices and other related offences in government organisations,[271] has revealed that 60% of their corruption cases are procurement related.[272]

MDAs and bureaus of public procurements are being accused of not adhering to due processes when selecting bidders and evaluating documentation to determine eligibility. This may result in the award of contracts to companies or 'ghost' companies which are incapable of delivering the contract according to approved specification, with the intent to unlawfully divert public funds for personal gain. This decay is deep-rooted as these procurement crimes are perpetrated by both senior and junior personnel in public offices. One of such top-profile cases is that of the directors-general of Securities and Exchange Commission, Mounir Gwarzo, and the National Health Insurance Scheme, Dr. Usman Yusuf, who were suspended on the grounds of alleged financial recklessness relating to violations of procurement law.[273] There was also the case of *FRN v Dr. Okechukwu Odunze & 6 or*,[274] where the defendants allegedly awarded contracts without approval and cash backing on the approved contract sum with intent to divert public funds. The weak implementation of procurement laws has contributed immensely to the deterioration of public utilities and public services[275] thus allowing for corrupt practices to thrive in the award of public contracts.

---

[269] Emmanuel Onwubiko, Weak Public Procurement Breeds Corruption (*The Guardian*, 07 March 2018) https://guardian.ng/issue/weak-public-procurement-breeds-corruption/ accessed 23rd May, 2018

[270] https://efccnigeria.org/ accessed 23rd May, 2018

[271] http://icpc.gov.ng/ accessed 23rd May, 2018

[272] Emmanuel Onwubiko, Weak Public Procurement Breeds Corruption (*The Guardian*, 07 March 2018) https://guardian.ng/issue/weak-public-procurement-breeds-corruption/ accessed 23rd May, 2018

[273] Ibid.

[274] A/1C/2013

[275] Emmanuel Onwubiko, n272

6

APPLICABLE COMMON LAW, LEGAL FRAMEWORK AND BEST PRACTICES

For stakeholders to tackle the challenges affecting alternative options of public service delivery, an assessment of applicable laws which can empower stakeholders to monitor the management of the private companies offering public services to ensure financial transparency, due diligence, compliance, accountability and public interest as they fulfill their contractual duties on public service delivery. The implementation is no doubt essential for the sustenance of public governance in the private sector.

Public and Private Partnerships

The paradigm shift in the monopolistic public enterprise to enable any government facing fiscal deficit to undertake public projects through private sector financing gave rise to the idea of Public Private Partnerships (PPP).[276] PPP represents a legal arrangement involving private investment in public projects and/or public co-financing of private projects that are in the public interest.[277] PPP agreements are designed as a form of contract; they may cover financing, construction, management, renovation and maintenance of

---

[276] John Forrer, James Edwin Kee, Kathryn E. Newcomer & Eric Boyer, Public-Private Partnerships and the Public Accountability (2010) 70 (3) *Public Administration Review* 475

[277] EICTDA, *Guidelines to Implement Public-Private Partnerships (PPP) Projects* http://www.mcit.gov.et/web/english/businesses/-/asset_publisher/GHgkYEVdqO97/document/id/1287048 accessed 26th April 2017

infrastructure. Such contracts range from short-term management contracts to concession contracts, joint ventures and partial privatisation,[278] as well as service contracts, and management contracts,[279] among others. Whatever form the PPP contract takes, it must involve the sharing of ownership between the government and private sector.[280]

In Nigeria, the federal and state governments have engaged in various PPP agreements to promote economic growth through improving the availability, quality and efficiency of power, water, transport and other public services.[281] The Infrastructure Concession Regulatory Commission (ICRC) has the mandate to take custody of every concession agreement made under the enabling Act and to monitor compliance with the terms and conditions of such agreement, among other functions.[282] The Infrastructure Concession Regulatory Commission (Establishment, ETC) Act, (ICRC Act)[283] and the National Policy on Public Private Partnership[284] were put in place to regulate the activities and monitor the management, supervision and execution of PPP agreements to ensure adherence to applicable laws or rules. Some sections of the ICRC Act provide for accountability measures; for example, sections 10 & 12 give the Federal Government and its agencies the power to inspect ongoing infrastructure projects while section 20 provides that the Commission will carry out duties necessary to ensure efficient execution of any concession agreement. Detailed perusal of both the Act and the policy guidelines indicate inadequacies, as key parameters for measuring accountability, disclosure and transparency in PPP project execution are absent.

The dynamics for public accountability in PPP are not exactly the same as the public sector because of the involvement of private partners. This is

---

[278] Ibid. See also Infrastructure Concession Regulatory Commission (Establishment, ETC) Act Cap A2 LFN 2004

[279] Abdulhamid Ozohu-Suleiman and Lawal Abdullahi Oladimeji, Public-Private Partnership and Infrastructural Development in Nigeria: The Rail Transportation Sector in Focus (2015) 7 (4) *British Journal of Education, Society & Behavioural Science*, 260

[280] EUR-Lex Access to European Union Law, *Green Paper on public-private partnerships* (2006) http://eur-lex.europa.eu/legal-content/EN/TXT/?uri=uriserv%3Al22012 accessed 24th August, 2017

[281] ICRC, *The National Policy on Public Private Partnership* http://www.icrc.gov.ng/resources/ publications/ accessed 26th August 2017

[282] ICRC, *What We Do* http://www.icrc.gov.ng/about-icrc/what-we-do/ accessed 26th August 2017

[283] ICRC Publications http://www.icrc.gov.ng/resources/publications/ accessed 26th April 2017

[284] Ibid.

because the purposes for the involvement of the government and the private partner differ;[285] the former aims to provide affordable public service and the latter seeks to generate profit.[286] This creates a complex situation for the stakeholders as they do not have adequate regulatory support to monitor the financial activities in a PPP project. Like the public sector, accountability, transparency and regulatory compliance in PPP projects and services are yet to be optimally achieved.

In Lagos State, the private sector is engaged by the state government as seen in the Lagos State PPP project on waste management through various agreements which have evolved over time.[287] Presently, waste management is governed through a policy (Clean Lagos Initiative (CLI))[288] backed up by law (Environmental Management and Protection Law)[289] to guide the PPP agreement between the Lagos State Government (Lagos State Ministry of Environment) and a private company (Municipal Contractors Waste Management Limited-MCWML).[290] Unfortunately, the PPP agreement on waste management between the Lagos State government and the MCWML (a conglomerate made up of foreign and local waste management firms) has been criticised for a number of reasons. However the discussion will be limited to unfair bidding processes and lack of accountability.

Unfair Bidding Process

On August 11th, 2016, the Lagos State government through the Ministry of Environment placed a two-page advert for invitations by way of expression of interest (EOI) for private sector investment in solid waste management by

---

[285] Posner Paul , Accountability Challenges of Third-Party Government in Lester M. Salamon (ed) *The Tools of Government: A Guide to the New Governance* (Oxford University Press,2002) 523

[286] Jeffrey N. Buxbam and Iris N. Ortiz, Protecting the Public Interest: The Role of Long-Term Concession Agreements for Providing Transportation Infrastructure (2007) 13 (2) *Keston Institute for Public Finance and Infrastructure Policy* 126

[287] Each newly elected government engage Private Sector Participants (PSP) through various agreements or contracts.

[288] http://www.cleanerlagos.org/ accessed 4th July, 2018

[289] Environmental Management Protection Law 2017

[290] This is a consortium made up of five companies: AVERDA, VEOLIA, SUZ, VISION SCAPE and ABC Sanitation.

the Lagos State Government. [291] The advert required that interested applicants would effectively perform the following waste management functions: collecting, transporting, processing and disposing waste generated in Lagos. Interested applicants were required to submit applications for any of the following categories of work:

(1) Residential and Street Waste Collection and Processing (Project No: MOE/SWM/0001): Applicants shall provide state of the art machinery and equipment; be paid a service fee on a monthly basis by the Lagos State government; take over the rehabilitation, upgrade and management of the three transfer loading stations in Lagos State; and undertake the establishment of a new transfer loading station.

(2) Provision of Engineered Sanitary Landfill: Applicants must provide the state of the art machinery and equipment to carry out the service under the project; and take over, rehabilitate, upgrade and manage the landfill sites in Lagos State on a Build Operate and Transfer (BOT).

(3) Secondary and Tertiary Drainage Management (Project No: MOE/SWM/0002): Applicants must provide state of the art machinery and equipment to carry put the contract; be paid a service fee on a monthly basis by the Lagos State Government.

To be eligible, applicants were required to possess and satisfy a number of requirements some of which are: provide evidence of professional and technical qualification to carry out the particular procurement; provide evidence of financial capacity to carry put the project; provide evidence of professional and technical staff/experience of key personnel of the company; provide evidence of similar projects undertaken by the applicant; provide audited accounts for the last three years; provide evidence of local presence with business offices; provide evidence of a minimum of 100 full time staff capable and available to carry out the project. The closing date for submission for proposal application was 26th August 2016.

After the publication was made, several Private Sector Participants (PSPs) of waste management in Lagos State expressed their dissatisfaction on the unfair eligibility requirements which disqualified all existing PSPs.[292] Their

---

[291] Punch Newspaper (August 11, 2018) see Appendix

[292] Ben Ezeamalu, How to Solve Lagos Waste Crisis–PSP Operators (*Punch*, 28th Feb 2018) https://www.premiumtimesng.com/regional/ssouth-west/260100-solve-lagos-waste-crisis-psp-operators.html accessed 10th July 2018

dissatisfaction and criticisms were hinged on the eligibility requirement violations of the Lagos State Public Procurement Law (LSPPL) 2012[293] and the regulatory forbearance of the Lagos State Public Procurement Agency (LSPPA).[294] One of the objectives of LSPPA is to ensure that bidding requirement *create ample opportunities for the citizenry, particularly small and medium scale enterprises, to participate in the economic opportunities and benefits of public procurement*.[295] Furthermore, the LSPPA are mandated to ensure they *attain transparency, competitiveness, professionalism and guarantee integrity and public trust in the public procurement procedure*.[296] An analysis of the bidding requirements as advertised suggest that the LSBPP neglected to adopt measures suitable for equal participation of PSPs to benefit from public procurement. Clearly, the LSPPA failed in their responsibility and failed to create ample opportunities for PSPs which operate as SMEs. Moreover, the PSPs expressed the dissatisfaction on the conscious sidelining of PSPs in favour of a foreign company, Visionscape which was awarded the solid waste management contract based on the actions which occurred before the invitation for proposals were advertised by the Lagos State Government.[297]

Prior to the advert by Lagos State Government, an unnamed environment sanitation firm based in Lagos had advertised for vacancies for sanitation managers in a national daily.[298] A few months after the unsigned advert was placed, the Lagos State government advertised for invitations for proposals for waste management.[299] The PSPs believed the Visonscape placed the unsigned advert based on a prior knowledge of the bidding requirements, thus giving

---

[293] Lagos State Public Procurement Law 201 https://nigerialii.org/ng/other/Lagos%20State%20 Public%20Procurement%20Law%202012.pdf accessed 10th July 2018

[294] Nigeria Infrastructure Advisory Facility, *PPP Manual for Lagos State Office of Public–Private Partnership* (2012) https://ppp.worldbank.org/public-private-partnership/sites/ppp.worldbank. org/files/documents/Lagos%20State_PPPManualFinal.pdf accessed 11th July 2018

[295] Lagos State Public Procurement Law n298 s8 (4)

[296] Ibid. s 8 (6)

[297] Nicholas Ibekwe, INVESTIGATION: How Lagos Gov't Sidelined Local Operators for Foreign Company with No Experience in Waste Collection, *PremiumTimes* (April 2, 2018) https://www. premiumtimesng.com/news/headlines/263725-investigation-how-lagos-govt-sidelined-local- operators-for-foreign-company-with-no-experience-in-waste-collection.html accessed 1th July 2018

[298] This advert was placed on *The Guardian Newspaper* (Thursday, May 5th 2016) See appendix for this advert;

[299] Punch Newspaper (August 11, 2018) See Appendix

it an unfair advantage over PSPs.[300] Although Visionscape neither confirmed nor denied this statement, LSBPP is yet to investigate whether Visionscape actually placed the advert to determine if the LSPPL was violated.[301] Although the veracity of the PSPs assumptions are yet to be determined, the LSPPL prohibits any direct or indirect attempt to influence the procurement process to obtain an advantage in the award of procurement contracts.[302]

A critical evaluation of section 22 (1) (a) & (b) of the Lagos State Public Procurement Law provides that '*all procurements carried out by any procuring entity shall be governed by the following rules: (a) Open Competitive bidding using clearly defined criteria, and offering to every interested bidder equal information and opportunities to offer the works, goods and services needed; (b) promotion of competition, economy, efficiency and equal opportunities to all parties who are eligible and qualified to participate in public contracts*' this suggest the Lagos State government through the Ministry of Environment did not provide opportunities for PSPs to offer the work needed. This is based on the short period bidders were allowed to submit all necessary documents; the bidding advert was placed on August 11th 2018 and the closing date for application submission was August 26th 2018, eleven (11) days after the advert placement. Such a short period did not give interested PSPs applicants the opportunity to restructure their activities to meet up with the proposal eligibility requirements. Interested PSPs, being SMEs with an average staff strength of 30–40 employees, did not have adequate time for possible mergers or re-structuring to make them eligible. Section 32 (4) of LSPPL, which provides that the LSBPP shall issue guidelines for the advertisement/ publication of Invitations to Bid, is not expressly defined. This creates loopholes for manipulative and sharp practices which may hamper the aim of section 22 (1) (a) which provides that all bidders should have equal information and opportunity. Although section 32 (2) & (3) expressly defines six (6) weeks as the duration for invitation for bids advertised on the notice board of the procuring entity and the State Procurement Journal for submission of the bids for the goods, works and services, in practice this cannot be deemed as adequate. This is based on the limited access to the LSBPP notice board and state procurement journal by a significant percentage of the general public.

The award of the waste management contract to Visionscape—an international environment sanitation firm—implies that the bidding is

---

[300] Nicholas Ibekwe n302

[301] Lagos State Public Procurement Law n298 s10 (1) (b) & (c)

[302] Ibid. s 70 (2) (e)

international and competitive. As required by section 32 (2) of LSPL, an international competitive bidding process *'shall be advertised in at least two (2) national newspapers, one (1) relevant internationally recognized newspaper, the official website of the procuring entity, the Agency and the State Procurement Journal not less than six (6) weeks before the deadline for submission of the bids for the goods, works and service'.* The advert for the EOI which initiated the PPP contract between the Lagos State Government and Visionscape contravened this section as the invitation for EOI was advertised in one (1) instead of two (2) national newspapers as required by the LSPL. In the event of a breach of a provision of the LSPPL in the procurement process, the LSBPP is mandated to recommend to the Governor the suspension, removal, discipline, temporary transfer or sanction of officers concerned in the procurement proceeding.[303]

Accountability

The PPP concession contract for waste management was awarded to Visionscape. Subsequently, Visionscape created a Special Purpose Vehicle (SPV) to form a conglomerate named Municipality Waste Management Contractors Limited (MWMCL) to finance the acquisition and development of a waste management infrastructure by strategically partnering with four companies (AVERDA, VEOLIA, SUZ, ABC Sanitations).[304] These companies have a long operational track record of performance in waste collection, waste treatment, waste recycling and waste energy to deliver an extensive and sustainable waste management system[305] which became the PPP partner with Lagos State for solid waste management.[306]

---

[303] Lagos State Public Procurement Law n299 s 10 (2)

[304] Global Rating Company, *GCR Accords An Indicative Rating of A(NG) To Municipality Waste Mgt. Contractors Ltd's N27bn Note* (9th June 2017) http://globalratings.com.ng/news/article/gcr-accords-an-indicative-rating-of-ang-to-municipality-waste-mgt.contracto accessed 12th July 2018

[305] Ibid.

[306] Gloria Ehiaghe and Chigozirim Enyinnia, Lagos Woos Investors for N50b Waste Bond, *The Guardian* (14th August 2017) https://guardian.ng/business-services/money/lagos-woos-investors-for-n50b-waste-bond/ accessed 11th July 2018; Visionscape, *Private Sector Plan N50bl Corporate Green Bond to Finance #Cleanerlagosinitiative* https://www.visionscape-sanitation.com/private-sector-plan-n50bl-corporate-green-bond-to-finance-cleanerlagosinitiative/ accessed 11th July 2018

The funding for the PPP concession is being raised by MWMCL through the issuance of a 50 billion Naira Notes Issuance Program in partnership with the Lagos State Government for investors to raise 50 billion Naira through a corporate green bond.[307] This bond is being guaranteed by the Lagos State through a 10 year Irrevocable Payment Standing Order (IPSO) to cover both coupon payments and principal redemption to ease MWMCL access to raised funds.[308] The ISPO serves as an agreement between the Lagos State and the MWMCL, which obligates the Accountant-General of the State to transfer funds monthly to the Sinking Funds Account (SFA). Thus the sum of 714 million will be transferred monthly into the SFA for the purpose of settling obligations under the Notes.[309] The ISPO is linked to the Lagos State revenue account and is valid for 10 years, commencing from June 2017 to June 2027.[310] This implies that the Lagos State Government will pay all outstanding liabilities in the event of termination of contract.

Usually, PPP contracts are financed by the private sector partner and not the government.[311] However, the government may finance a PPP concession if the project on its own merit cannot achieve bankability, financial viability or is otherwise exposed to specific risks that the private investors is not well placed to manage.[312] One of the eligibility requirements for the Lagos State Government invitation for proposal advert for waste management was that each applicant must provide evidence of financial capacity to carry out any of the project categories.

It is also imperative to note that the justification for engaging the private sector to fully undertake waste management was centred on the Lagos State Government's inability to fund the high cost of waste management through the Lagos State Waste Management Agency (LAWMA).[313] This initiated a

---

[307] Gloria Ehiaghe Ibid.

[308] Global Rating Company, n310

[309] Ibid.

[310] Ibid.

[311] Nigeria Infrastructure Advisory Facility, *PPP Manual for Lagos State Office of Public-Private Partnership* (2012) https://ppp.worldbank.org/public-private-partnership/sites/ppp.worldbank.org/files/documents/Lagos%20State_PPPManualFinal.pdf accessed 11th July 2018

[312] World Bank, *Government Support in Financing PPPs* https://ppp.worldbank.org/public-private-partnership/financing/government-support-subsidies accessed 12th July 2018

[313] Bola Badmus, Ambode Halts LAWMA from Waste Bill Collection, Approves 100% Payment to PSP Operators, *Tribune* (26th January 2017) http://www.tribuneonlineng.com/58442/ accessed 12th July 2018

reform which changed the status of LAWMA, a waste management agency, to a regulatory agency.[314] Thus, the decision by the Lagos State Government to assist MWMCL in raising funds and guaranteeing same through SFA and ISPO questions the ... of reason for outsourcing waste management to the private sector on the reason of unavailability of funding. This implies that the Lagos State Government will absolve consequent financial risks and liabilities arising from the PPP concession, thereby absolving Visionscape of any risks in the PPP concession contract.

ISPOs are oftentimes used by corrupt government officials as instrument to siphon public funds in tranches through porous contracts facilitated through breach of procurement processes.[315] Generally, procurement laws provide for prerequisites or conditions precedents such as submission of certificate of completion, or fulfillments of the specific terms of the contract before payments are made to a procuring entity or before an ISPO is initiated to offset government financial obligation.[316] However, public procurement fraud or non-adherence to due process allows for these conditions to be subverted. For instance, the efficiency and capability of MCWML has come under the scrutiny, resulting the unanticipated waste management crises in Lagos State resulting from poor sanitation on the roads, sewage and waste collection.[317] This prompted the petitioning for an investigation by the Civil Society Network against Corruption (CSNAC) to the Economic and Financial Crimes Commission (EFCC) for allegations of economic fraud, incompetence and dubious dealings by MCWML.[318] Unfortunately, neither LAWMA nor

---

[314] Ibid.

[315] Rasheedat A. Okoduwa, *Aspects of Corrupt Practices in Public Sector Procurement* (paper delivered at a 2-day Workshop on Public Sector Procurement and Financial Management, Wednesday, 22nd July 2011) http://icpc.gov.ng/wp-content/uploads/downloads/2013/05/ASPE CTS-OF-CORRUPT-PRACTICES-IN-PUBLIC-SECTOR-PROCUREMENT.doc accessed 11th July 2018

[316] Lagos State Government Lagos State Public Procurement Agency (PPA), *Procurement Regulations* 2014, Rule 141-145 https://lagosppa.gov.ng/regulations/ accessed 7th August 2018

[317] Nicolas Ibekwe, INVESTIGATION: How Lagos Gov't Sidelined Local Operators for Foreign Company with No Experience in Waste Collection *PremiumTimes* (April 2nd 2018) https://www.premiumtimesng.com/news/headlines/263725-investigation-how-lagos-govt-sidelined-local-operators-for-foreign-company-with-no-experience-in-waste-collection.html accessed 10th July 2018; Olasunkanmi Akoni, LAGOS REFUSE: How We're Transiting Waste into Next Phase *Vanguard* (1 February 2018) https://www.vanguardngr.com/2018/02/lagos-refuse-transiting-waste-next-phase-irvine-ceo-visionscape/ accessed 11th July 2018

[318] http://csnacng.org/demand-for-the-investigation-of-the-ownership-of-visionscape-sanitation-solutions-and-its-contract-with-the-lagos-state-government/ accessed 20th August 2018

LSBPP are yet to exercise their function as a regulator to sanction MCWML for inefficiency in waste management in Lagos State. Similarly, in Plateau and Bayelsa States,[319] over the sum of 64 billion and 30 billion Naira respectively were siphoned through ISPOs, and Commission reports suggest that contracts tied to ISPOs are all in a deplorable state or abandoned, yet payments were being made to the private companies contracted to provide these services.[320] In *EFCC v Bala James Ngiliari & ors*,[321] the defendant Bala Ngiliari, a former Executive Governor of Adamawa State was convicted of public procurement fraud. The accused awarded a contract to El-Yadi Motors Limited for the supply of 25 units of Toyota Camry at sum of one hundred and sixty seven million eight hundred thousand and twelve thousand, five hundred naira (N167, 812,500.00) without obtaining a 'No Objection' certificate and other necessary documentations provided in the Adamawa State Bureau of Public Procurement laws before initiating payments. Award of government contracts not hinged on any service or product is a corrupt practice that has eaten deeply into the fabric of the public sector in Nigeria. In *EFCC v Raymond Dokpesi*,[322] the defendant was on trial for receiving the sum of two billion one hundred and twenty million (N2,120,000,000.00) from the National Security Agency (NSA) without delivering any service or product to the federal government or any of its agencies. In *EFCC v Olugbenga Obadina &ors*,[323] the defendant was charged with receiving the sum of two billion, four hundred and seventeen million naira (N2,417,000,000.00) in tranches through his company Almond Project Limited for a bogus contract which did not require the supply of any goods or services to the office of the National Security Adviser.

---

[319] These are two of the thirty-six States in Nigeria

[320] Taye Obateru, Mabas Akila and Omawumi Tuoyo, Nigeria: 64 Billion Naira Siphoned Through Irrevocable Standing Payment Orders, Commission Told, *Vanguard* (17 September, 2008) http://allafrica.com/stories/200809170482.html accessed 4th July 2018; Francis Agbo, The Road less travelled *Vanguard* (5th April 2012) https://www.vanguardngr.com/2012/04/governor-dickson-the-road-less-travelled-2/

[321] https://efccnigeria.org/efcc/news/2681-efcc-to-appeal-acquittal-of-ex-adamawa-gov-ngilari accessed 8th August 2018

[322] FHC/ABJ/CR/380/2015

[323] http://efccnigeria.org/efcc/news/2090-n2-4bn-onsa-contract-scam-how-obadina-mismanaged-funds-witness accessed 9th July 2018

The Economic Confidential report on the insolvency of several States[324] can be attributed to their substantial debt.[325] A significant degree of these debts are incurred through public procurement corruption. Public procurement corruption is significant because procurement accounts for the largest share of public expenditure at all tiers of government.[326] Where a State's public procurement regulatory mechanism is lax, especially if the corrupt practices are being perpetrated by the Governors or top procurement officers, as in the Bala James Ngiliari case, ISPO become instruments for syphoning public funds. Besides the insolvency risk exposure, this significantly impacts negatively on the development of public services and infrastructures because public funds released for specific improvement or provision of public services and infrastructure which are never delivered.

Tackling bribery, corruption and self-interest is a centre-stage problem for private companies that offer public services. The complexities of PPP contracts and public procurement may hamper stakeholders' ability to monitor breach of trust, fiduciary duties and corrupt practices. In order to address this challenge, stakeholders should have an authoritative guidance on specific legal framework which accords them legal rights and protection effective for monitoring breach of trust, fiduciary duties and corrupt practices. The applicable legal framework of focus to this paper are: common law, FOI Act and Companies and Allied Matters Act.

Common Law

Under the Nigerian legal system, stakeholders are accorded legal protection under the common law and statutes from liabilities or injuries arising from damages emanating from the breach of a statutory duty. There are fundamental difference to these two remedies, as Lord Wright in *LPTB v Upson*[327] succinctly

---

[324] Economic Confidential, A*SVI 2017: 36 States Generate N931bn IGR Against N3.3trn from Federation Account* (April 28th 2018) https://economicconfidential.com/2018/04/asvi-36-states-igr-2017/ accessed 10th July 2018; Yakubu Dati, Lalong Unveils Path to Prosperity, *Vanguard* (April, 9th 2017) https://www.vanguardngr.com/2017/04/lalong-unveils-path-prosperity/ accessed 10th July 2018

[325] Budget IT, *The State of States* (Budget IT, 2015) http://yourbudgit.com/wp-content/uploads/2016/01/THE-FATE-OF-STATES-Final1.pdf accessed 10th July 2018

[326] Rasheedat A. Okoduwa, n320

[327] [1949] A.C. 155

explains:

> '*a claim for damages for breach of a statutory duty intended to protect a person in the position of a particular plaintiff is a specific common law right which is not to be confused in essence with a claim for negligence. The statutory right has its origin in the statute, but the particular remedy of an action for damages is given by the common law in order to make effective, for the benefit of the injured plaintiff, his right to the performance by the defendant of the defendant's statutory duty. It is an effective sanction. It is not a claim in negligence in the strict ordinary sense... Whatever the resemblances, it is essential to keep in mind the fundamental differences of the two classes of claim*'.

Under this common law principle, stakeholders can claim for damages against a company or government agency if there is a breach of statutory duty. To succeed in this claim, it must first be proved that a duty of care is owed by the government or the private company.[328] In establishing this, stakeholders must establish that there was a duty of care by proving: that there is a relationship of proximity between the parties; that an injury to the claimant was foreseeable; that it is fair, just and reasonable to impose a duty.[329] Once this is established, stakeholders must prove that the duty of care was breached. In considering this, the court may consider the following: the capacity of the defendant, the cost and difficulty of the defendant taking precautionary measures, the extent of the potential risk to the claimant, the seriousness of any likely injury, state of knowledge and industry standards, among others.[330] Thereafter, the stakeholders must prove that the negligent action of the defendant caused or made a material contribution to their injuries. In deciding this, the court will consider if the chain of causation was broken by an intervening act or event.

---

[328] LexisNexis, *Proving Negligence or Breach of Statutory Duty* https://www.lexisnexis.com/uk/lexispsl/personalinjury/synopsis/448:449/Establishing-legal-liability/Proving-negligence-or-breach-of-statutory-duty?wa_origin=gnb accessed 21st May 2018

[329] LexisNexis, *Practice Notes: Who Owes Duty of Care?* https://www.lexisnexis.com/uk/lexispsl/personalinjury/document/393875/55MK-3WF1-F18H-M0F6-00000-00/Who_owes_a_duty_of_care_ accessed 21st May 2018

[330] LexisNexis,, *Practice Notes: Did the Breach of Duty Cause Damage?* https://www.lexisnexis.com/uk/lexispsl/personalinjury/document/393875/55MK-3WF1-F18H-M194-00000-00/Did_the_breach_of_duty_cause_damage_ accessed 21st May 2018

Lastly the stakeholders must prove that the injury was foreseeable.[331]

Under common law, stakeholders are compensated for any liability or damage incurred from a PPP project. The court iterated this in *Adeshina v Lemomu*,[332] where the court held that 3rd parties have the right to invoke tortious liability such as negligence, nuisance and trespass to challenge a government project arising from the breach of duty under common law or by statute. The court iterated that under a PPP project, a 3rd party must prove that the project caused him a particular damage over and above that suffered by the general public which occurred as a result of an interference with a public right in order to succeed in such claim.

Freedom of Information Act:

In order to evaluate the practices and affairs of a private company, stakeholders may need access to the records of the company to identify the directors, shareholders, objective and powers of the company, among others. The FOI Act gives stakeholders the right to request for information listed in the FOI Act from '*all corporations established by law, and all companies in which government has a controlling interest, and private companies utilizing public funds, providing public services or performing public functions*'.[333] This means that private companies are not excluded from the FOI Act provided they utilize government funds, provide public services or perform public functions. This accords stakeholders the same level of rights the FOI Act offers for public institutions.

Companies and Allied Matters Act (CAMA)[334]

Private or public listed companies registered under the Corporate Affairs Commission (CAC) which provide public services on behalf of the government must adhere to the provisions of the CAMA. CAMA makes provision for the

---

[331] LexisNexis, *Practice Notes: Was the damage foreseeable?* https://www.lexisnexis.com/uk/lexispsl/personalinjury/document/393875/55MK-3WF1-F18H-M0F0-00000-00/Was_the_damage_foreseeable_ accessible 21st May 2018

[332] [1965] 1 All NLR 233

[333] Freedom of Information Act 2011 n 21 s2(7)

[334] Companies and Allied Matters Act, Cap LFN 2004

incorporation of companies and incidental matters. One of such incidental matters is the duties of directors. These duties are a response imposed to balance the unfettered powers and freedom of directors to ensure a minimum standard of behaviour to prevent directors shrouding their transactions in secrecy,[335] or acting in a manner contrary to the interest of the company.[336] The duties of directors broadly categorised as fiduciary duties and statutory duties. Fiduciary duties of directors were developed from equitable principles and duties of skill and care emanating from the principles from laws of trusts and agency[337] and common law.[338] Statutory duties are provided through enacted laws.[339]

Fiduciary duty is the highest standard of care.[340] Directors must carry out their duties within the organisation with the highest standard of care. Director's duty of care emanates from the legal principle of care whereby an individual is made liable for negligence which results in harm to someone else.[341] The duty of care and skill is a mandatory statutory requirement for directors. Therefore, the exercise of their powers and discharge of their duties must be done in good faith with a high degree of care, diligence and skill that a reasonable prudent director would exercise in comparable circumstances.[342] This duty extends to delegated duties as directors are not always absolved from deficiencies or liabilities incurred by the company even though the duties were delegated to another staff of the company.[343]

The CAMA makes specific provisions for directors' duties, and most relevant is the provision of section 279 (1), (3) & (8) which provides:

(1) A director of a company stands in a fiduciary relationship towards the company and shall observe the utmost good faith towards the company in any transaction with it or on its behalf.

(3) A director shall act at all times in what he believes to be the best interests of the

---

[335] John Farrer, *Farrer's Company Law* (2nd edn, Butterworths 1988) 324

[336] Alan Dignam & John Lowry, *Company Law* (5th den, Oxford University Press, 2009) .302

[337] Ibid. 298

[338] Birds J. & Boyles A.J., *Boyle &Birds' Company Law* (6th edn, Jordan Publishing, 2007) 605

[339] Companies and Allied Matters Act n334

[340] Legal Information Institute, *Fiduciary Duty* https://www.law.cornell.edu/wex/fiduciary_duty accessed 14th July 2018.

[341] Sarah Worthington, Reforming Director's Duties (2001) 64 (3) *Modern Law Review* 439–458

[342] Companies and Allied Matters Act n334 s282

[343] *Adebayo v Johnson* (1969) All NLR, 171

company as a whole so as to preserve its assets, further its business, and promote the purposes for which it was formed, and in such manner as a faithful, diligent, careful and ordinarily skilful director would act in the circumstances.

(8) No provision, whether contained in the articles or resolutions of a company, or in any contract shall relieve any director from the duty to act in accordance with this section or relieve him from any liability incurred as a result of any breach of the duties conferred upon him under this section;

Traditionally, directors owe these duties to the company and not to individual shareholders, and employees.[344] This was established in the *Percival v Wright* case where Swinfen Eady J stressed that to extend the duties of directors to other actors would place directors *'in a most invidious position.'* However, this decision has been greatly criticised owing to its limitations when interpreting the phrase *'interest of the company'* as provided in section 279 (3) in a pluralist context. The fiduciary duties of directors to other actors of the company such as: shareholders, creditors and other stakeholders of the company are now being recognised by the courts if the circumstance demands that a fiduciary obligation of a director can be established.[345] Although these provisions can only be enforced against the director(s) by the company,[346] public stakeholders can petition the Corporate Affairs Commission to take appropriate legal action against a director(s) of companies providing public services who do not act in the interest of the public are brought to justice. As provided in section 7 (a) & (c) the Commission is mandated to:[347]

(a) ...administer this Act including the regulation and supervision of the formation, incorporation, registration, management, and winding-up of companies under or pursuant of this Act;

(c) arrange or conduct an investigation into the affairs of any company where the interest of the shareholders and the public so demand;

---

[344] *Percival v Wright* [1902] 2 Ch 421; Ibid. s 279 (1)
[345] *Nicholson v Permakraft* (NZ) Ltd [1985] NZLR 242
[346] Companies and Allied Matters Act, n334 s279 (9)
[347] Ibid.

Class action

Though CAMA does not specifically give right to stakeholders[348] which will accord public sector stakeholders the right to sue a company or its directors, members of the public (community) directly affected by the operations of a private company can bring a class action against the company. Class action is an effective mechanism to remedy mass wrong.[349] A class action ensures that a defendant who engages in a widespread harm which on an individual ratio is minimal against each individual plaintiff, must compensate those individuals for their injuries.[350] Most significantly, class action can be used to change the behaviour of a class of which the defendant is a member.[351] In *Landeros v. Flood*[352] the general reluctance of doctors to report child abuse was changed after a civil action for damages was instituted against the defendant for the failure to report the suspected child abuse as required by law. As Chief Justice Warren Burger opined, '*The aggregate of individual claims in the context of a class wide suit is an evolutionary response to the existence of injuries unremedied by the regulatory action of the government. Where it is not economically feasible to obtain relief within the traditional frame work of a multiplicity of small individual suits for damages, aggrieved persons may be without any effective redress unless they employ the class action device...*'[353] The institution of class action in Nigeria depends on the procedural rules which are the federal[354] and state high court civil procedural rules.[355] Unfortunately, both the federal and state high court rules limit the scope of applicability of class action by providing specific instances a class action can be brought before the court. Generally, class action can be brought under any of the following

---

[348] With exception to creditors and regulators

[349] Douglas Martin, The Rise and Fall of the Class-Action Lawsuit (*NY TIMES* Jan. 8, 1998) at B7

[350] Uche Obi, *Understanding Class Action Litigation As Tool For Ventilating Mass Grievance,* Paper presented at the NBA Conference Port Harcourt 2016 http://www.alliancelf.com/wp-content/uploads/2018/03/Understanding-Class-action-Litigation-as-tool-for-ventilating-Mass-Grievance-with-amendment-FINAL-REVIEW.pdf accessed 23rd July 2018

[351] Ibid.

[352] 17 cal. 3d 399

[353] *Deposit Guar. Nat'l Bank V. Roper*, 44 US 326,339,338 n.9 (1980)

[354] http://edojudiciary.gov.ng/wp-content/uploads/2016/10/Federal-High-Court-Civil-ProcedureRule.pdf accessed 23rd July 2019

[355] Each of the 36 States in Nigeria enacted its own Civil Service Rules.

subject matters: Intellectual property, Environmental, Security, Employment, Consumer fraud/Product liability, Customary Law or Community Land, Property subject to Trust and Construction of statute or instrument among others.

Corporate governance

Private companies registered under CAMA are not mandated to observe the Securities and Exchange Commission's (SEC)[356] code of corporate governance in addition to the provisions of CAMA. However, they are encouraged to apply its principles where appropriate. In the wake of poor public service delivery, and with the level of public interest vested in these private companies by the government which may have destructive consequences on the welfare of the citizens, mandating private companies which offer public services to observe the SEC code of corporate governance should be a key point for consideration. To justify this consideration, the concept of corporate governance should be understood. Corporate governance promotes '*a fair, efficient and transparent administration to meet certain well-defined objectives...through a system of structure... with a view to achieve long-term strategic goals to satisfy shareholders, creditors, employees, customers and suppliers, and complying with the legal and regulatory requirements, apart from meeting environmental and local community needs*'.[357] Considering that the major reason for the introduction of corporate governance was as a result of corporate failures and scandals which was as a result of corrupt practices which led to widespread corporate failures,[358] good corporate governance practices could promote financial transparency, regulatory compliance, and best practices which reduces investors risks while protecting the interests of its stakeholders.

In context, the SEC code responsibilities will be discussed to the extent it prescribes measures which minimise the risk of private companies being used as an avenue to divert public funds. To facilitate this, it is imperative for this code to have an obligatory clause for: responsibilities of the board

---

[356] *Securities and Exchange Commission Code of Corporate Governance For Public Companies* 2011 http://sec.gov.ng/ accessed 8ᵗʰ August 2018

[357] Corporate governance: Time for a Metamorphosis, The Hindu Line quoted in N. Gopalsamy, Corporate Governance: Introduction in N. Gopalsamy (ed.) *A Guide to Corporate Governance* (Newage Publishers, 2008) 20

[358] Ibid. p.21

of directors, conflict of interest, relationship with stakeholders, and a whistle blowing policy.[359]

Board of Directors:[360] To ensure accountability and performance of the company's set objectives, the board must define the company's strategic goals and ensure that availability and efficiency of its human and financial resources are effectively deployed towards attaining those goals. It is the responsibility of the Board to oversee the effective performance of the company's businesses to meet its legal obligations to its employees and other stakeholders. This entails high ethical standards of compliance to its articles and memorandum of association, as well as public procurement contracts, CAMA among others. The Board must define a framework for the delegation of its authority or duties to Management specifying matters that may be delegated and those reserved for the Board. The responsibility of the board will not be diminished, as the Board remains accountable and responsible for the affairs of the company. An effective policy and programme for reporting issues such as corruption and general corporate social responsibility must be developed by the Board.

Conflict of Interest:[361] In context, this challenge arises when there are speculations that the company and its director(s) are mere agents of the government with the main purpose of providing an avenue for diversion of public funds. Hence if directors are required to develop and enforce specific SEC corporate governance provisions on conflict of interest and provide proof of compliance, challenges posed by conflict of interest will be minimised. An effective policy which will significantly abate conflict of interest must embody strict provisions which will make both the culpable director criminally responsible and the Board collectively responsible through a pecuniary fine on a strict liability basis for undisclosed conflict of interest. For the strict liability to apply, the culpable director need not make secret profit. Liability can arise on the grounds of non-disclosure of a perceived or real conflict.

Directors who are aware of a real, potential or perceived conflict of interest of a fellow director have a responsibility to promptly raise the issue for clarification, either to the Board or with the Chairman of the Board. Any question on the existence of real or perceived conflict must be determined by the Board by vote.

---

[359] SEC code of Corporate Governance for Public Companies n356
[360] Ibid. Part B
[361] Ibid. s16

Relationship with Stakeholders: This remains the bedrock of both corporate governance and public governance. As the SEC code provides, '*Companies should pay adequate attention to the interests of its stakeholders such as its employees, host community, the consumers and the general public...should demonstrate sensitivity to Nigeria*'s social and cultural diversity and should as much as possible promote strategic national interests as well as national ethos and values without compromising global aspirations where applicable.'[362] In application, private companies may have limited powers to adhere to this provision because they are bound by the terms of the awarded contract. However, in executing the contract '*...directors must commit themselves to transparent dealings and to the establishment of a culture of integrity and zero tolerance to corruption and corrupt practices*'.[363] The Board must develop policies for public reporting of social, ethical and environmental practices in its business operations which may include[364] implemented strategies for past businesses which reflect compliance to relevant ethical standards, as well as application of the company's codes of practice in its operations which stipulating its impact on the society and environment, among others.

Whistle Blowing: Effective policies which establish a confidential mechanism for employees, directors and the public to report illegal and unethical behaviour of the officers and employees of the company must be established and maintained by a reputable third-party. This will significantly aid in curbing corruption. Such a requirement will make it difficult for government officials to liaise with company directors to divert public funds meant for public services.

Compliance to these responsibilities should be compulsory and must be audited by an independent third-party firm which will rate each company's compliance level and make necessary advice for approval or issuance of a certificate of compliance by SEC. This certificate should be one of the prerequisites for any private company that intends to bid for contracts from the government to provide public services. This presents prima facie evidence that the board of directors is accountable, observes ethical standards, complies to issues of conflict of interest, and is effective in the performance of its duties.

The certificate of compliance issued by SEC must have strict separate legal implications which will make the Board of Directors criminally liable

---

[362] Ibid. Part D

[363] Ibid. Part D (28.2)

[364] Ibid. Part D (28.3)

if a certified private company is charged with public procurement fraud. In addition to the SEC compliance certificate, private companies must adopt measures which identifies with the OECD corporate governance report[365] applicable for the advancement of public governance best practices within private companies.[366] This report recognises the nexus between the interests of stakeholders and performance of a company, with a view to promoting economic efficiency, sustainable growth and sound financial management.[367] This must be seen as incorporated into the company's polices and code of practice for its business operations and must essentially prescribe practices which recognise the role of stakeholders and its linkages with communication, disclosure and transparency.[368]

---

[365] The six OECD corporate governance principles are: ensuring the basis for an effective corporate governance framework; the rights and equitable treatment of shareholders and key ownership functions; institutional investors, stock markets, and other intermediaries; the role of stakeholders; disclosure and transparency; and responsibilities of the board

[366] OECD, *Principles of Corporate Governance: OECD* Report to G20 Finance Ministers and Central Bank Governors (2015) p.10 https://www.oecd.org/daf/ca/Corporate-Governance-Principles-ENG.pdf accessed 28th August 2017

[367] Ibid..

[368] Ibid.

7

ENFORCEMENT OF PUBLIC GOVERNANCE

Enforcing public governance in Nigerian public institutions is a two-way responsibility. On the one hand, the management of public institutions are duty-bound to implement and maintain practices that promote public governance principles through best practices, governance principles and applicable laws. On the other hand, stakeholders are also bound to monitor compliance and performance in public service organisations based on specific provisions of the FOI Act, CAMA and best practice guidelines. Owing to its interdependent nature, stakeholders may face challenges in achieving public governance if the corresponding roles of public institutions are not fulfilled. Unlike the FOI Act, non-mandatory governance principles are non-binding since they simply present guidelines on best practices[372] for the improvement of a legal and regulatory framework.[373]

Role of Public Institutions

This paper identifies two core components which public institutions must possess to advance public governance: good governance structure and a prolific citizens' participation model.

---

[372] Australian Stock Exchange (ASX), *Corporate Governance Council's Principles of Good Corporate Governance and Best Practice Recommendation of 2003* http://www.asx.com.au/2003/index.html accessed 10th February 2015

[373] OECD, n366

Good Governance: This is the bedrock of performance in public institutions and the cornerstone for efficient and effective organisational performance which is reinforced by a number of principles.[374] According to the Auditor General of British Colombia,[375] as well as the Government of Western Australia,[376] some of the principles which underpin a good governance structure in the public sector are accountability, leadership, ethics and integrity, stewardship, transparency, organisational structure, operational planning, human resource development, financial management, as well as open and responsive communication.

Incorporating these principles into policies for periodic human development staff training, policy development in financial reporting, organisational structure reforms and in any other area will considerably promote public governance. The management and employees of public service organisations have the task of continuously self-appraising in order to ensure that relevant and operational good governance measures are entrenched in all spheres of public administration. The OECD toolkit for public governance suggests ways this can be achieved:[377]

i.   Strategic Planning: The organisation's management should design operational and administrative plans that will focus on leadership, ethics and a culture committed to good public-sector governance.

ii. Culture: Management should entrench a culture of compliance, integrity, commitment to service delivery and transparency, strict compliance to legal and regulatory obligations, together with internal policies focused on creating a good governance structure. This can be achieved through incentives that encourage employees to adhere to the culture of compliance.

iii. Performance Assessment: Before the management establishes internal staff assessment procedures for performance monitoring and evaluation,

---

[374] Australian National Audit, *Public Sector Governance: Strengthening Performance Through Good Governance* (2014) https://www.anao.gov.au/work/better-practice-guide/public-sector-go vernance-strengthening-performance-through-good accessed 18th April 2017

[375] Ibid.

[376] Government of Western Australia PSC, *Good Governance Guide for Public Sector Agencies* (2013) https://publicsector.wa.gov.au/public-administration/public-sector-governance/good-governance-guide-public-sector-agencies accessed 18th April 2017

[377] OECD, *Policy Framework For Investment User's Toolkit: Public Governance* (2012) p 18 http://www.oecd.org/investment/toolkit/policyareas/publicgovernance/41890394.pdf accessed 17th August 2017

both management and employees should be educated on public governance principles. This can be achieved through periodic trainings and specialised courses for human resource development.

iv. Internal Review and Evaluation of Governance Arrangement: Management should periodically assess the performance of public governance measures to determine their effectiveness in improving public service delivery.

v. Consultation Mechanism: An open and transparent procedure for effective and timely inputs through public (stakeholders) consultations is essential. The aim is to increase efficiency and effectiveness by identifying poorly designed or weakly applied policies, with a view to ensuring that investments are productive and the quality of public service is improved. It is also an effective means to ensure that quality public service standards are maintained through direct feedback.

Citizens' Participation/Stakeholders Enagagement: According to the UN World Public Sector Report, citizens' participation implies '... *the involvement of citizens in a wide range of policymaking activities, including the determination of levels of service, budget priorities, and the acceptability of physical construction projects in order to orient government programs toward community needs, build public support, and encourage a sense of cohesiveness within neighborhoods.*'[378]

Citizen participation is achieved through various models which provide blueprints for public sector organisations to effectively engage civil societies by facilitating communication between government agencies, citizens and other interest groups regarding a specific decision or public issue.[379] The impact of citizen participation is momentous, and it is being utilised by governments around the globe to achieve effective public service administration. With over fifty-four (54) models of citizens' participation, different jurisdictions adopt a model ideal for achieving meaningful involvement of citizens in public sector administration. For instance, the IAP 2 spectrum model specifies five levels of government/participant engagement and expected outcomes: informing, consulting, involving, collaborating, and empowering to engage citizens'

---

[378] UN Public Administration Program, *The Role of Active Participation and Citizen Engagement in Good Governance* (2013) http://www.un.org/esa/socdev/egms/docs/2013/EmpowermentPolicies/Elia%20Armstrong%20presentation.pdf accessed 31st July 2018

[379] Ortwin Renn, Thomas Webler, Peter Wiedmann, *Fairness and Competence in Citizens Participations: Evaluating Models for Environmental Disclosure* (Kluwer Academic 1995) p.2

participation.[380] With the IAP 2 model, the least level of citizen engagement is to provide a platform to share information to assist public understanding of a complex issue. At the *'consult'* level, feedback is obtained from participants on proposed government decisions. The next level of citizens' engagement is *'involve'*. This provides a platform which actively collects stakeholder feedback for the express purpose of ensuring that stakeholder concerns are considered by governments. The next level of engagement is *'collaborate'*. This facilitates direct communication between government and the public. The highest and final level is *'empower'*. At this level, decisions offered by participants through a platform are implemented in practice. Most developed jurisdictions such as, Australia, Lebanon, USA, and Canada and among others adopt the IAP 2 model to promote and sustain citizens' participation.[381]

Citizens' participation models are being adopted beyond public service administration and politicians are increasingly engaging members of the public through citizen's participation based initiatives. For instance, in the United Kingdom politicians are increasingly engaging the public in democratic processes and politics through various initiatives.[382] The Labour Government has deployed this concept to significantly promote public sector reforms through new structures and initiatives, leading to significant development in the local National Health Services (NHS), new transport service routes and improved police relationship with the communities.[383] Also, the Local Strategic Partnership (LSP) initiative has influenced most communities by creating formal and informal social connections between service providers and the communities they serve.[384] In Nigeria, public service organisations are yet to adopt citizens' participation models or implement policies which promote citizens' participation. Consequently, there is no recognised platform

---

[380] Matti Nelimarkka, Brandie Nonnecke & Sanjay Krishnan et al, *Comparing Three Online Civic Engagement Platforms Using the "Spectrum of Public Participation" Framework* http://goldberg. berkeley.edu/pubs/oxford-ipp-2014-spectrum.pdf accessed 1st September 2018

[381] IAP2, *2015 IAP2 Federation Year in Review* https://iap2usa.org/resources/Documents/Fede ration/2015iap2yearinreview.pdf accessed 1st September 2018

[382] Paul Skidmore, Kristen Bound & Hannah Lownsbrough, *Community Participation: Who Benefits* (Joseph Rowntree Foundation, 2006) http://www.jrf.org.uk/system/files/1802-comm unity-network-governance.pdf accessed 19th May 2016

[383] Ibid.

[384] Kath Maguire and Frances Truscott, *The Value Added by Community Involvement in Governance* (Joseph Rowntree Foundation July 2006) http://www.jrf.org.uk/publications/value-added-community-involvement-governance accessed 19th May2016

for communication between the public and public service organisation officials in making substantive decisions on matters concerning their community.[385] The inability of the citizens to dialogue with officials on specific public service issues significantly contributes to the implementation challenges of the FOI Act and poor service delivery.

Role of Stakeholders

Stakeholders' role in ensuring compliance to public governance principles can be achieved in various ways, one of which is coalition of stakeholders and community participation. As a developing economy, major challenges affect public service such as undue political influences which fosters corruption and poor public service delivery. Coalition of stakeholders and community participation are ideal tools which stakeholders can utilize to tackle undue political influence and pressure the government to conform to their needs.

Coalition of Stakeholders: Coalition can be defined as '*self-conscious, freely-organized, active and lasting alliances of elites, organizations, and citizens sharing partially overlapping political goals.*'[386] Coalition is a collaboration of individuals to realize a shared objective in order to attain a common goal.[387] Coalition of stakeholders provides a shared platform for like-minded groups leveraging on the collective force of their members to amplify their voices to build support for a specific cause.[388] Coalitions serve different purposes and have been formed in various ways. In governance and public administration, it is formed to pressurise the government and its agencies to change their policies to conform to the needs of stakeholders or implement a reform.

To increase the effectiveness and success of a coalition, pertinent factors must be put in place by the coalition initiators. Firstly, the objective for the coalition must be defined and significant actors or core members identified

---

[385] Nancy C. Robert, Direct Citizen Participation in Roberts N. C. (ed.) *The Age of Direct Citizens Participation* (Sharpe 2008) p.7

[386] Sahr Kpundeh, *Strategy for Coalitions' as Quoted in CommGAP*, 'Coalition Building' http://siteresources.worldbank.org/EXTGOVACC/Resources/CoalitionBuildingweb1.pdf accessed 6th August 2018

[387] CommGAP Ibid.

[388] Ellis Planning Associates, *Engaging Diverse Stakeholders in Coalition* (Jan. 2011) http://ellisplanningassociates.com/engaging-diverse-stakeholders-in-coalitions-2/ accessed 17th April 2017, See also CommGAP ibid

through stakeholder mapping.[389] The categorisation of stakeholders requires assessment of significant factors such as: resources, legal framework, socio-economic and cultural characteristics of the core members, as well as ideology and knowledge of key relevant issues[390] which must be considered to demonstrate credibility and ensure adequate representation. This is vital for the purposeful expansion and sustainable transformation of the coalition, which are critical if the coalition must retain its coherence and effectiveness. Most successful pro-reform coalition building efforts in jurisdictions such as Kenya (Water Sector Reform Secretariat (WSRS)),[391] Philippines (Transparent Accountable Governance (TAG)),[392] India (Public Enterprise Reform (PER))[393] recognised and implemented these key issues which aided in the achievement of their set objectives. In Nigeria, the coalitions of stakeholders are yet to achieve notable strides in public sector reforms. The fundamental challenge could be the lack of capacity to form a viable stakeholder organisation, or lack of capacity of existing stakeholder organisations to cater for cross-purposes, which in context is public service reform. In the recent past, the most notable forms of coalition of stakeholders are political in nature and operate sporadically through peaceful demonstrations to express public dissatisfaction at government policies or actions. Some notable groups/ NGOs are the Bring Back Our Girls Campaign, One Voice Nigeria, and

---

[389] CommGAP n 385

[390] Tina Nabatchi, *Building Coalition and Partnership through Stakeholders Engagement* http:// gpsaknowledge.org/wp-content/uploads/2014/11/Nabatchi-Stakeholder-Engagement.pdf accessed 6th August 2018

[391] George O. Khroda, A Consensus-Based, Stakeholder-Driven, and Decentralized Approach to Building Broad Coalitions for Water Sector Reforms in Sina Odugbemi & Thomas Jacobson (eds.) *Governance Reform Under Real-World Conditions: Citizens, Stakeholder, and Voice* (World Bank, 2008). http://siteresources.worldbank.org/EXTGOVACC/Resources/GovReform_ebook. pdf accessed 10th July 2018

[392] Robert de Quelen, Building Pro-Change Multisectoral Coalitions to Overcome the Resistance of Powerful Vested Interests in Sina Odugbemi & Thomas Jacobson (eds.), *Governance Reform Under Real-World Conditions: Citizens, Stakeholder, and Voice* (World Bank, 2008) http:// siteresources.worldbank.org/EXTGOVACC/Resources/GovReform_ebook.pdf accessed 10th July 2018

[393] Steve Masty, Communication, Coalition Building, and Development: Public Enterprise Reform in West Bengal and Orissa States, India' in Sina Odugbemi & Thomas Jacobson (Eds.), *Governance Reform Under Real-World Conditions: Citizens, Stakeholder, and Voice* (World Bank, 2008) 355–389 http://siteresources.worldbank.org/EXTGOVACC/Resources/GovReform_ebook.p df acccessed 10th July 2018

Occupy Nigeria. If public service stakeholders are to achieve a sustainable and viable coalition, the coalitions' set objectives and strategies should be flexible and sustainable to advance public sector reforms with strategic plans of advancing public governance. The core actors of the coalitions should be organised groups or NGOs which are knowledgeable in public service capable of engaging other stakeholders for cross-purposes. The coalition's core actors should have knowledge of key issues affecting public governance advancement, and must have the ability to identify challenges while being experienced in strategic engagement of government agencies to conform to public governance principles. Like the ALPE of Georgia,[394] which was set up specifically to advance the communication programme for the Judiciary by several NGOs, if necessary a new organisation can be specifically formed to advance a specific public governance programme. Ideally, local authorities should organize meetings with stakeholders in the form of town hall meetings to, among others, discuss intended development work, provide assurance on initiatives that improve public service, promote knowledge sharing, and discuss new initiatives which should be flexible and adaptive. As Emezi rightly has observed, the local government is a *'system of local administration under local communities that are organized to maintain law and order, provide some limited range of social amenities, and encourage cooperation and participation of inhabitants towards the improvement of their conditions of living'.*[395] The core purpose of the local government is to promote the well-being and quality of life of citizens through efficient performance of functions and delivery of services.[396] The local government, also known as the grassroots government, was created to bring government closer to the people.[397] It provides the

---

[394] Jose-Manuel Bassat 'Building Support for the Rule of Law in Georgia' in Sina. Odugbemi & Thomas Jacobson (Eds.), *Governance Reform Under Real-World Conditions: Citizens, Stakeholder, and Voice* (World Bank, 2008)

[395] Emezi, Cleus, 'Local Government in Historical Perspective' (1984) 2(2) *Nigerian Journal of Public Administration and Local Government,* 50

[396] Aderonke Majekodunmi, The State of Local Government and Service Delivery in Nigeria: Challenges and Prospects (2012) *Africa's Public Service Delivery and Performance Review* https://www.researchgate.net/publication/320377280_The_State_of_Local_Government_and_ Service_Delivery_in_Nigeria_Challenges_and_Prospects accessed 8th August 2018

[397] Ozohu-Suleiman Abdulhamid & Paul Chima, Local Government Administration in Nigeria: The Search For Relevance (2015) 18 Commonwealth *Journal of Local Governance,* 48

most basic of public services: health, transportation, and sanitation etc.[398] The efficacy of the local government can be assessed by the quality of public service available within a local community. This is because the main goal of the local government is to improve government's productivity and enable the local community to participate in their social, political and economic governance.[399] Unfortunately, in Nigeria over the years local governments have largely failed in their responsibilities and in some regions can be described as absent since they are unable to make a difference in community development. This is as a result of lack of autonomy which creates challenges such as poor government funding, lack of human capital, corruption, and ultimately poor public service delivery. If properly organised, community participation can significantly impact on the local government and public service providers, leading to improvements in the quality of basic social amenities for a specific geographical area. Community participation means that individuals and families assume responsibility for decisions that affect their welfare and the development of their community. This requires all stakeholders to express their opinion on matters affecting their community. It is particularly effective in influencing government policies at the local government level.

---

[398] College of Public Affairs and Community Services, *Local Government* https://www.unomaha. edu/college-of-public-affairs-and-community-service/public-administration/academics/mpa-concentration-local-government.php accessed 7th August 2018

[399] Abugu, S.O, The Role And Challenges of Local Government In Community Development: An Insight (2014) 3(6) *Review of Public Administration and Management*, 131

8
CONCLUSION

The unsatisfactory outcomes of previous and present civil service reforms clearly depict the shortcoming of a non-citizens' centred reform. Public sector reform is an arduous task, which can only be satisfactorily achieved through a correlated strategy between the government and the citizens. Public administration and management is ever changing and is deeply affected by changing social values, political ideologies, as well as public service demands and expectations. Public governance creates an avenue which allows for easy adaptation to changes in public service demands through the involvement of public stakeholders.

The role of stakeholders in public administration and governance is too important to be ignored. The concept of shared responsibilities between stakeholders and the government in public administration and governance has gained support globally as a result of widespread corruption and poor public service delivery in the public sector. The concept of public governance depicts interdependence between the governments and public, which may be difficult to achieve in public service administration within the Nigerian context. Nevertheless, the Nigerian public service is fast progressing into a contracting state as public service productivity and service delivery are adversely affecting the economy, public health and safety, and international perception of economic development. Thus, the inevitable interdependence between public institutions and stakeholders must be acknowledged and enforced.

Although this work focuses on the role of stakeholders in promoting public governance, the role of the management of public institutions is no doubt critical. One major factor which contributes to ineffective implementation of the FOI Act is the absence of a citizens' participation model in public service organisations. The adoption and implementation of a citizens' participation model is crucial for public governance. Public service organisations can utilize, where applicable, the UN Division of Public Administration and Development Management (UN DPADM) Open Government Data and Citizen Engagement Toolkit. This toolkit provides a blueprint for strategies which public institutions can adopt for opening government data and citizen engagement. The toolkit can be implemented in coordination with the FOI Act and an ideal citizens' participation model.

The FOI Act has been illustrated as an indispensable tool for public service reform which expressed the duality of its application to both public institutions and private companies which offer public services. Like most public right centred legislation, the onus to enforce its provisions rests on the public and not the government, as it requires strategic coalition of stakeholders.

The impact of the private sector firms which offer public services on behalf of the government is highly underestimated and in most cases not fully considered for public service reform. This contributes significantly to its poor monitoring in public service performance evaluation. Owing to the impact of private companies in public service delivery, it is mandatory that a model governance code be established which will address key issues for the advancement of public governance. Unlike the SEC Code of corporate governance, compliance to the model governance code must be mandatory for effective results.

Quite pertinent is the need for a review of the CAMA to incorporate modern company law principles which recognise the need to establish a director and stakeholder relationship similar to the United Kingdom's Company Act. Likewise, the FOI Act should be amended to specifically stipulate its applicability to all thirty-six (36) States in Nigeria.

There are simply no short cuts, public sector stakeholders have a role to play to ensure that the principles of public governance are implemented to improve public service delivery and accountability.

TABLE OF CASES

R v Inhabitants of the County of Bedfordshire (1855) 24 L.J.Q.B. 81 at 84

Re Eccleston and Department of Family Services (1993) 1 QAR 60

Re Heaney v The Public Service Board (1984) 6 ALD 310

Uzeogwu F.O.C Vs CBN & the Attorney General of the Federation FHC/ABJ./CS/1016/2011 (Unreported)

Waterson v Lloyd [2011] EWHC 3197

Securities and Exchange Commission Code of Corporate Governance for Public Companies 2011

TABLE OF LEGISLATION

BIBLIOGRAPHY

Abdulhamid O. & Chima P., Local Government Administration in Nigeria: The Search for Relevance (2015) 18 *Commonwealth Journal of Local Governance*

Abugu O., The Role And Challenges of Local Government In Community Development: An Insight (2014) 3(6) *Review of Public Administration and Management*

Adekoya A., Corporate Governance Reforms in Nigeria: Challenges and Suggested Solutions (2011) 6 (1) 38 *Journal of Business Systems, Governance and Ethics* http://www.jbsge.vu.edu.au/issues/vol06no1/Adekoya.pdf accessed 7th October 2016

Afolayan A., *A Critical Analysis of the Freedom of Information Act in Nigeria* (2012) https://odinakadotnet.wordpress.com/2012/08/01/a-critical-analysis-of-freedom-of-information-act-in-nigeria-2/ accessed 13th July 2016

Agbo F., The Road Less Travelled *Vanguard* (5th April, 2012) https://www.vanguardngr.com/2012/04/governor-dickson-the-road-less-travelled-2/ accessed 10th July 2018

Aidan R., *Results-Orientated Budget Practice in OECD Countries* (Overseas Development Institute Working Paper, 2003) https://www.odi.org/sites/odi.org.uk/files/odi-assets/publications-opinion-files/2035.pdf accessed 24th August, 2017

Akoni O., LAGOS REFUSE: How We're Transiting Waste Into Next Phase *Vanguard* (1st February 2018) https://www.vanguardngr.com/2018/02/lagos-refuse-transiting-waste-next-phase-irvine-ceo-visionscape/ accessed 11th July 2018

Alfred N., Public Administration and the Development of Africa: A Critical Assessment (2016) 6 (1) *Journal of Public Administration and Governance*

Angelopoulos K., Philippopoulos A. & Tsionas E., *Does Public Sector Efficiency Matter? Revisiting The Relation Between Fiscal Size and Economic Growth in a World Sample* (2008) https://www.gla.ac.uk/media/media_43670_en.pdf accessed 19th March 2018

Anozode R., Okoye J. & Chukwuemeka E., Civil Service Reforms in Nigeria:

The Journey So Far in Service Delivery, (2013) 3 (1) *American Journal of Social and Management Sciences*

Arowolo D. & Ologunowa C., Privatisation in Nigeria: A Critical Analysis of the Virtues and Vices (2012) 1(3) *International Journal of Development and Sustainability*

Asiedu E., Foreign Direct Investment in Africa: The Role of Natural Resources, Market Size, Government Policy, Institutions and Political Instability (2006) 29 *The World Economy*

Audit Commission, *Trust in the Public Sector* www.auditcommission.gov.uk accessed 17th April 2016

Audit Commission, *Corporate Governance: Improvement and Trust in Local Public Service* (2003) http://archive.auditcommission.gov.uk/auditcommission/sitecollectiondocuments/AuditCommissionReports/NationalStudies/CorporateGovernance.pdf accessed 14th April 2016

Audit Commission, *Creating Public Value: An Analytical Framework for Public Service Reform* (Strategy Unit, Cabinet Office, November 2002) http://archive.audit-commission.gov.uk/auditcommission/subwebs/publications/studies/studyPDF/3126.pdf accessed 9th October 2017

Australian Information Commissioner, *FOI Guidelines* https://www.oaic.gov.au/freedom-of-information/foi-guidelines/ accessed 27th September 2017

Australian National Audit, Public Sector Governance: Strengthening Performance Through Good Governance (2014) https://www.anao.gov.au/work/better-practice-guide/public-sector-governance-strengthening-performance-through-good accessed 18th April 2017

Australian National Audit Office, *Public Sector Governance* https://www.anao.gov.au/sites/g/files/net616/f/2014_ANAO%20-%20BPG%20Public%20Sector%20Governance.pdf accessed 24th August 2017

Australian Public Service Commission, *Building Better Governance* http://www.apsc.gov.au/__data/assets/pdf_file/0010/7597/bettergovernance.pdf accessed 24th August 2017

Australian Public Services Commission, *The Australian Experience of Public Sector Reform*, (2015) http://unpan1.un.org/intradoc/groups/public/documents/apcity/unpan021316.pdf accessed 4th April 2017

Australian Stock Exchange, *Corporate Governance Council's Principles of Good Corporate Governance and Best Practice Recommendation of 2003* http://www.asx.com.au/2003/index.html accessed 10th February 2015

Baderin M., Law and Development in Africa: Towards a New Approach' (2011) 1 NIALS *Journal of Law and Development*

Badmus B., Ambode Halts LAWMA from Waste Bill Collection, Approves 100% Payment to PSP Operators *Tribune* (26th January 2017) http://www.tribuneonlineng.com/58442/ accessed 12th July 2018

Bangura Y., *Ethnic Inequalities and Public Sector Governance* (2006, Palgrave)

Bayo O., Federal Civil Service Reform in Nigeria: The Case of Democratic Centralism' (2012) 1(10) *Journal of Radix International Educational and Research Consortium*

Beach S., Brown K., Keast R., Together Now: Stakeholders in Government Agencies (*International Research Society for Public Management Conference*, Brisbane, 2008)

Bhavsar H., Significance and Relevance of Proactive Disclosure in the Implementation of RTI Act (2015) 2 (5) *International Journal of Allied Practice, Research and Review*

Birkinshaw P., Freedom of Information (4th edn, Cambridge Press 2010)

Boin A., & Christensen T., The Development of Public Institutions: Reconsidering the Role of Leadership (2008) 40 *Administration and Society*

Bourgon J., Responsive, Responsible and Respected Government: Towards a New Public Administration Theory (2007) 73 (1) 7 *International Review of Administrative Sciences*

Birds J. & Boyles A.J., Boyle & Birds' Company Law (6th edn, Jordan Publishing, 2007)

Borins S., New Public Management, North American Style, in Kathleen McLaughlin, Stephen Osborne and Ewan Ferlie (eds.) *The New Public Management: Current Trends and Future Prospects* (Routledge, 2000)

Bovaird T., Developing New Forms of Partnership with the Market in the

Procurement of Public Services (2006) 84 *Public Administration*

Bureau of Public Service Reforms (BPSR), *Public Service Reforms in Nigeria 1999-2014 A Comprehensive Review* (2015)

Budget IT, *The State of States* (Budget IT, 2015) http://yourbudgit.com/wp-content/uploads/2016/01/THE-FATE-OF-STATES-Final1.pdf accessed 10th July 2018

Buxbam J. & Ortiz I., Protecting the Public Interest: The Role of Long-Term Concession Agreements for Providing Transportation Infrastructure' (2007) 13 (2) *Keston Institute for Public Finance and Infrastructure Policy*

Cabinet Office, *The UK Government's Approach to Public Service Reforms* (2006) http://webarchive.nationalarchives.gov.uk/20070701080507/cabinetoffice.gov.uk/strategy/downloads/work_areas/public_service_reform/sj_pamphlet.pdf accessed 4th April 2017

Cadbury Committee (U.K.), *Report of the Committee on the Financial Aspects of Corporate Governance*, (1992) http://cadbury.cjbs.archios.info/report 22nd March 2018

Chandler J., Public Administration: A Discipline in Decline, (1991) 9 *Teaching Public Administration*

Cleus E., Local Government in Historical Perspective (1984) 2(2) *Nigerian Journal of Public Administration and Local Government*

College of Public Affairs and Community Services, Local Government https://www.unomaha.edu/college-of-public-affairs-and-community-service/public-administration/academics/mpa-concentration-local-government.php accessed 7th August 2018

Cornforth C., *The Governance of Public and Non-profit Organisations. What Do Boards Do?* (2003, Routledge)

Dati Y., Lalong Unveils Path To Prosperity *Vanguard* (April, 9th 2017) https://www.vanguardngr.com/2017/04/lalong-unveils-path-prosperity/ accessed 10th July 2018

Darma N. & Ali M., An Assessment of Public Sector Service Delivery In Nigeria: A Case Study of Federal Capital Territory Area Councils 2007–2011 (2014) 3(8) *International Journal of Development and Sustainability*

Dickinson H., From New Public Management to New Public Governance: The Implications for a New Public Service in John Butcher and David Gilchrist (eds.) *The Three Sector Solution: Delivering Public Policy In Collaboration with Not-For-Profits and Business* (ANU, 2016)

Dickinson H., *Performing Governance: Partnerships, Culture and New Labour* (Macmillan, 2014)

Dignam A. & Lowry J., *Company Law* (5ᵗʰ edn, Oxford University Press, 2009)

Economic Confidential, *ASVI 2017: 36 States Generate N931bn IGR Against N3.3trn from Federation Account* (April 28ᵗʰ 2018) https:// economicconfidential.com/2018/04/asvi-36-states-igr-2017/ accessed 10ᵗʰ July 2018

Edwards M. & Clough R., *Corporate Governance and Performance: An Exploration of the Connection in a Public Context* (Issues Series Paper No 1, January 2005) http://www.canberra.edu.au/corpgovaps/pub/Issues PaperNo.1_GovernancePerformanceIssues.pdf

Edwards M., Halligan J., et al, *Public Sector Governance in Australia* (Australian National University E-Press, 2012) http://press-files.anu.edu. au/downloads/press/p190701/pdf/preliminary.pdf accessed 5ᵗʰ April 2018

Ehiaghe G. & Enyinnia C., Lagos Woos Investors for N50b Waste Bond *The Guardian* (14 August 2017) https://guardian.ng/business-services/ money/lagos-woos-investors-for-n50b-waste-bond/ accessed 11ᵗʰ July 2018

Ellis Planning Associates, *Engaging Diverse Stakeholders in Coalition* (Jan, 2011) http://ellisplanningassociates.com/engaging-diverse-stakeholders-in-coalitions-2/ accessed 17ᵗʰ April 2017

EICTDA, *Guidelines to Implement Public - Private Partnerships (PPP) Projects* http://www.mcit.gov.et/web/english/businesses/-/asset_publisher/GHgk-YEVdqO97/document/id/1287048 accessed 26ᵗʰ April 2017

Evans A., *Civil Service and Administrative Reform: Thematic Paper* (IEG Working Paper 2008)

EUR-Lex Access to European Union Law, *Green Paper on Public-Private Partnerships* (2006) http://eur-lex.europa.eu/legal-content/EN

TXT/?uri=uriserv%3Al22012 accessed 24th August 2017

Ezeamalu B., *How to solve Lagos Waste Crisis—PSP Operators Punch* (28th Feb. 2018) https://www.premiumtimesng.com/regional/ssouth-west/260100-solve-lagos-waste-crisis-psp-operators.html accessed 10th July 2018

Fagbohun L., Introduction to Law: Nigerian Legal System in Dapo F. Asaju (Ed.), *Readings in General Studies: Nigeria and African Studies* (2nd edn, LASU Press, 2006)

Farazmand A., Global Administrative Reforms and Transformation of Governance and Public Administration' in Ali Farazmand & Jack Pinkowski (eds.) *Handbook of Globalization, Governance & Public Administration* (1st edn Routledge, 2006)

Farnham D. & Horton S., Managing Private and Public Organisations' in Farnham D. & Horton S. (eds.) *Managing the New Public Services* (2nd edn, Macmillan, 1993)

Farrer J., Farrer's *Company Law* (2nd edn, Butterworths 1988)

Federal Ministry of Finance, *FMF—Whistle Blowing Frequently Asked Questions (FAQs)*, (2017) https://whistle.finance.gov.ng/_catalogs/mas terpage/MOFWhistle/assets/FMF%20WHISTLEBLOWING%20FREQU ENTLY%20ASKED%20QUESTIONS.pdf accessed 18th April 2017

Federal Ministry of Justice, *Guidelines on the Implementation of the Freedom of Information Act 2011* (FMJ, 2013) 16

Finn P., *Official Information: Integrity in Government* (Canberra, 1991)

Forrer J., Kee J.,Newcomer K. & Boyer E., Public-Private Partnerships and the Public Accountability (2010) 70 (3) *Public Administration Review*

Frederickson G. & Smith K., *The Public Administration Primer* (Westview Press, 2003)

Freeman E. & Reed D., Stockholders and Stakeholders: A New Perspective on Corporate Governance (1983) 25 *California Management Review*

Freeman J., The Private Role in Public Governance (2000) *New York University Law Review* 73 (3) 593

Fung B., The Demand and Need for Transparency and Disclosure in Corporate

Governance (2014) 2 (2) *Universal Journal of Management*

Garcia-Sanchez, I., Rodriguez-Dominguez, L. & Gallego-Alvarez, I. Effectiveness of Ethics Codes in the Public Sphere: Are They Useful in Controlling Corruption? (2011) 34 (3) *International Journal of Public Administration*

GCPSE, *From Old Public Administration to the New Public Service: Implications for Public Sector Reform in Developing Countries* (2015) http://www. undp.org/content/dam/undp/library/capacitydevelopment/English/Sing apore%20Centre/PS-Reform_Paper.pdf accessed 26th March 2018

Global Rating Company, *GCR Accords An Indicative Rating of A(NG) To Municipality Waste Mgt. Contractors Ltd's N27bn Note* (9th June 2017) http://globalratings.com.ng/news/article/gcr-accords-an-indicative-ratin g-of-ang-to-municipality-waste-mgt.contracto accessed 12th July 2018;

Gloteka, *Establishment of a Public Institutions* http://www.gloteka.lt/en/ public_institution accessed 4th July 2016

Gopalsamy N., Corporate Governance: Introduction in N. Gopalsamy (ed.) *A Guide to Corporate Governance* (Newage Publishers, 2008)

Government of Western Australia PSC, Public Sector Governance' https:// publicsector.wa.gov.au/public-administration/public-sector-governance 28th August 2017

Government of Western Australia PSC, Good Governance Guide for Public Sector Agencies' (2013) https://publicsector.wa.gov.au/public-administration/public-sector-governance/good-governance-guidepublic -sector-agencies accessed 18th April 2017

Harry H., *A Review of Private Approaches for Delivery of Public Services* (Urban Institute Press, 1983)

Hassan M., Corporate Governance Practices in Emerging Economies: Initial Findings From the UAE' (2011) 10 (9) *China-USA Business Review* http:// www.davidpublishing.com/davidpublishing/Upfile/10/17/2011/2011101 776035585.pdf accessed 14th April 2016

Hill C., & Jones T., Stakeholder-Agency Theory (1992) 29 (2) 133 *Journal of Management Studies* http://onlinelibrary.wiley.com/doi/10.1111/j.1467 -6486.1992.tb00657.x/pdf accessed 14th July 2016

Hood C., A Public Management for All Seasons? (1991) 69 *Public Administration*

Hong Kong Institute of Certified Accountants, Corporate Governance for Public Bodies: A Basic Framework' (May 2004) 4 http://app1.hkicpa. org.hk/publications/corporategovernanceguides/eframework_guide.pdf accessed 11ᵗʰ October 2016

IAP2, *2015 IAP2 Federation Year in Review* https://iap2usa.org/resources/ Documents/Federation/2015iap2yearinreview.pdf accessed 1ˢᵗ September 2018

Ibekwe N., INVESTIGATION: How Lagos Govt Sidelined Local Operators For Foreign Company with No Experience in Waste Collection *PremiumTimes* (April 2, 2018) https://www.premiumtimesng.com/news/ headlines/263725-investigation-how-lagos-govt-sidelined-local-operator s-for-foreign-company-with-no-experience-in-waste-collection.html accessed 1ˢᵗ July 2018

ICO Guidance, *Freedom of Information: Good Practice Guidance No.5* (2007) https://www.whatdotheyknow.com/request/119280/response/304644/at tach/3/ICO%20Guidance%20Internal%20Review%20Time%20Limits.p df accessed 7ᵗʰ September 2017

ICRC, *The National Policy on Public Private Partnership* http://www.icrc.gov. ng/resources/publications/ accessed 26ᵗʰ August 2017

ICRC Publications, http://www.icrc.gov.ng/resources/publications/ accessed 26ᵗʰ April 2017

ICRC, *What We Do* http://www.icrc.gov.ng/about-icrc/what-we-do/ accessed 26ᵗʰ August 2017

IDA, *Towards 2030: Investing in Growth, Resilience and Opportunity* (World Bank, 2017) http://documents.worldbank.org/curated/en/4717 61467993490105/IDA18-IDA18-overarching-theme-towards-2030-inves ting-in-growth-resilience-and-opportunity accessed 22ⁿᵈ March 2018

IFAD, *Good Governance: An Overview* (September, 1999) http://www.ifad. org/gbdocs/eb/67/e/EB-99-67-INF-4.pdf accessed 11ᵗʰ October 2016

IFAC, *Governance in the Public Sector: A Governing Body Perspective International Public Sector Study* (2001) 11 http://www1.worldbank.org/

publicsector/pe/befa05/Study_13_Governance.pdf accessed 22nd March 2018

Iyayi A., The Civil Service Reforms in Nigeria since Independence in Bello-Imam (ed.) *50 Years of the Nigerian Project: Challenges and Prospects* (College Press 2010) 247

Jarvis R., *The UK Experience of Public Administration Reform Current Good Practices and New Developments in Public Service Management* (Common Wealth Secretariat, 2002)

JISC Legal Information Services and Dundas & Wilson, *Freedom of Information and the Public Interest Test* (2004) http://www.humanrightsinitiative.org/programs/ai/rti/implementation/applying_law/public_interest_uk_jisc.pdf accessed 30th September 2017

Jumanne B. & Keong C., Foreign Direct Investment and Public Sector Management and Institutions: The Acquaintances in Sub-Saharan Africa (SSA) Low-Income Economies (2017) V (II) *African Journal of Economic Review*

Kettl D., *Sharing Power: Public Governance and Private Markets* (The Brookings Institution, 1993)

Khroda, G., A Consensus-Based, Stakeholder-Driven & Decentralized Approach to Building Broad Coalitions for Water Sector Reforms' in Sina Odugbemi & Thomas Jacobson (eds.) *Governance Reform Under Real-World Conditions: Citizens, Stakeholder & Voice* (World Bank, 2008) http://siteresources.worldbank.org/EXTGOVACC/Resources/GovReform_ebook.pdf accessed 10th July 2018

Kickert, W., Public Governance in the Netherlands: An Alternative to Anglo-American 'Managerialism', (1997) 75 (4) *Public Administration*

Kitchen, H., Delivering Local/Municipal Services in Anwar Shah (eds.) *Public Service Delivery* (World Bank, 2005.) 128 http://siteresources.worldbank.org/PSGLP/Resources/PublicServiceDelivery.pdf accessed 26th April 2018

Kpundeh S., *Strategy for Coalitions* as quoted in CommGAP, Coalition Building http://siteresources.worldbank.org/EXTGOVACC/Resources/CoalitionBuildingweb1.pdf accessed 6th August 2018

Kumar R., Changing Role of the Public Sector in the Promotion of Foreign

Direct Investment (2003) 10 (2) *Asia Pacific Development Journal*

Lähdesmäki, K., *New Public Management and Reforming Public-sector Management: A Study of the Principles of Organisational Efficiency, Economy and Effectiveness & Public Sector Entrepreneurship, Performance Management & their Accountability in Public Sector Management Reforms in Finland from the late 1980 to the Early 1990s* (University of Vasa, 2003)

Lee E. & Haque M., The New Public Management Reforms and Governance in Asian NICs: A Comparison of Hong Kong and Singapore (2006) 19 (4) *Governance*

Legal Information Institute, *Fiduciary Duty* https://www.law.cornell.edu/wex/fiduciary_duty accessed 14th July 2018

LexisNexis, Proving Negligence or Breach of Statutory Duty https://www.lexisnexis.com/uk/lexispsl/personalinjury/synopsis/448:449/Establishing-legal-liability/Proving-negligence-or-breach-of-statutory-duty?wa_origin=gnb accessed 21st May 2018

LexisNexis, *Practice Notes: Who Owes Duty of Care?* https://www.lexisnexis.com/uk/lexispsl/personalinjury/document/393875/55MK-3WF1-F18H-M0F6-00000-00/Who_owes_a_duty_of_care_ accessed 21st May 2018

LexisNexis, *Practice Notes: Did The Breach of Duty Cause Damage?* https://www.lexisnexis.com/uk/lexispsl/personalinjury/document/393875/55MK-3WF1-F18H-M194-00000-00/Did_the_breach_of_duty_cause_damage_ accessed 21st May, 2018

LexisNexis, Practice Notes: Was the damage foreseeable?' https://www.lexisnexis.com/uk/lexispsl/personalinjury/document/393875/55MK-3WF1-F18H-M0F0-00000-00/Was_the_damage_foreseeable_ accessible 21st May, 2018

Maathai W., *The Challenge for Africa: A New Vision* (William Heinemann, 2009)

Maguire K. & Truscott F., *The Value Added by Community Involvement in Governance* (Joseph Rowntree Foundation July 2006) http://www.jrf.org.uk/publications/value-added-community-involvement-governance accessed 19th May 2016

Majekodunmi A., The State of Local Government and Service Delivery in Nigeria: Challenges and Prospects (2012) 1 *Africa's Public Service Delivery and Performance Review* https://www.researchgate.net/publication/320377280_The_State_of_Local_Government_and_Service_Deliver y_in_Nigeria_Challenges_and_Prospects accessed 8th August 2018

Martin D., The Rise and Fall of the Class-Action Lawsuit *NY Times* (Jan. 8 1988) https://www.nytimes.com/1988/01/08/us/the-law-the-rise-and-fall-of-the-class-action-lawsuit.html accessed 12th July 2018

Marshall J. & Murtala A., Public Service in Nigeria- An Overview of Functions and Code of Conduct (2015) 3 (1) *Global Journal of Politics and Law Research*

Max C., A Stakeholder Framework for Analyzing and Evaluating Corporate Social Performance (1995) 20 *Academy of Management Review*

Media Rights Agenda, *A Citizen's Guide to the Freedom of Information Act 2011* (Media Rights Agenda 2011)

Metcalfe L. & Richards S., *Improving Public Management* (Sage, 1991)

Mischra R., *The Welfare State in Crisis* (Wheatsheaf, 1984)

Mulyadu M., The Importance of Corporate Governance in Public Sector (2012) 1 *Global Business and Economics Research Journal*

Nabatchi T., Building Coalition and Partnership through Stakeholders Engagement http://gpsaknowledge.org/wp-content/uploads/2014/11/N abatchi-Stakeholder-Engagement.pdf accessed 6th August 2018

Nelimarkka M., Nonnecke B. & Krishnan S., et al, *Comparing Three Online Civic Engagement Platforms using the 'Spectrum of Public Participation' Framework* http://goldberg.berkeley.edu/pubs/oxford-ipp-2014-spectru m.pdf accessed 1st September 2018

Nigeria Infrastructure Advisory Facility, *PPP Manual for Lagos State Office of Public-Private Partnership* (2012) https://ppp.worldbank.org/public-private-partnership/sites/ppp.worldbank.org/files/documents/Lagos%20 State_PPPManualFinal.pdf accessed 11th July 2018

Nwanolue, B. & Victor Iwuoha, The Nigerian Civil Service and Promotion of Sustainable Human Development: A Critical Analysis (2012)1 (9)

Arabian Journal of Business and Management Review

Obateru T., Akila M. & Tuoyo O., Nigeria: 64 Billion Naira Siphoned Through Irrevocable Standing Payment Orders, Commission Told *Vanguard* (17 September, 2008) http://allafrica.com/stories/200809170482.html accessed 4ᵗʰ July 2018

Obi U., *Understanding Class Action Litigation As Tool For Ventilating Mass Grievance* (Paper presented at the NBA Conference Port Harcourt 2016) http://www.alliancelf.com/wp-content/uploads/2018/03/Understanding-Class-action-Litigation-as-tool-for-ventilating-Mass-Grievance-with-am endment-FINAL-REVIEW.pdf accessed 23ʳᵈ July 2018

OECD, *OECD Principles of Corporate Governance* (OECD Publishing, 2004) p.11 https://www.oecd.org/corporate/ca/corporategovernanceprinciples /31557724.pdf accessed 4ᵗʰ Oct 2016

OECD, *Measuring and Improving Government Performance* http://www.oecd. org/site/worldforum06/38756317.pdf 19ᵗʰ March 2018

OECD, *Policy Framework for Investment User's Toolkit: Public Governance* (2012) p18 http://www.oecd.org/investment/toolkit/policyareas/publicg overnance/41890394.pdf accessed 17ᵗʰ August 2018

Ogbeidi M., Political Leadership and Corruption in Nigeria Since 1960: A Socio-economic Analysis' (2012) 1 (2) *Journal of Nigerian Studies*

Okoduwa R., *Aspects of Corrupt Practices in Public Sector Procurement* (paper delivered at a 2-day Workshop on Public Sector Procurement and Financial Management, Wednesday, 22ⁿᵈ July 2011) http://icpc.gov. ng/wp-content/uploads/downloads/2013/05/ASPECTS-OF-CORRUPT-PRACTICES-IN-PUBLIC-SECTOR-PROCUREMENT.doc accessed 11ᵗʰ July 2018

Okorie C. & Odo S., A Survey of Public Service Reforms in Nigeria: 1999–2013 (2014) 4 (10) *International Journal of Humanities and Social Science*

Osborne S., The New Public Governance? (2006) 8 (3) *Public Management Review* http://spp.xmu.edu.cn/wp-content/uploads/2012/12/the-New-Pu blic-Governance.pdf accessed 14ᵗʰ July 2016

Osborne S., The (New) Public Governance: A Suitable Case for Treatment? in Stephen Osbourne (ed.) *The New Public Governance? Emerging*

Perspectives on the Theory and Practice of Public Governance (Routledge, 2010)

Osborne S., Radnor Z. & Nasi G., A New Theory for Public Service Management? Towards a (Public) Service Dominant Approach (2013) 43 (2) *The American Review of Public Administration*

Olalekan M., Olayinka S. & Omotayo I., The Impacts of the Nigerian Civil Service Reforms on Effective Service Delivery (2016) VII *International Journal of Politics and Good Governance*

Olufemi J. & David K., Public Sector Reform in Africa: Issues, Lessons and Future Directions, (2010) 12 *Journal of Sustainable Development in Africa*

Olusegun O., *The Nigerian Legal System* (Sweet & Maxwell, 1979)

Onwubiko E., Weak Public Procurement Breeds Corruption *The Guardian* (7th March 2018) https://guardian.ng/issue/weak-public-procurement-breeds-corruption/ accessed 23rd May 2018

Orcan T., *Law in Aid of Development* (Ghana Publishing, 1978)

Parkinson J., Corporate Governance and the Regulation of Business Behaviour in Sorcha MacLeod (ed.) *Global Governance: a Quest for Justice* (Hart Publishing, 2006)

Patapas A., Raipa A., et al., New Public Governance: The Track of Changes (2014) 4 (5) *International Journal of Business and Social Research* http://www.researchgate.net/publication/272625263_New_Public_Governance_The_Tracks_of_Changes accessed 14th July 2018

Paul P., Accountability Challenges of Third-Party Government in Lester M. Salamon (ed) *The Tools of Government: A Guide to the New Governance* (Oxford University Press, 2002) 523

Peters G., Managing the hollow state' in K. A. Eliassen and J. Kooiman (eds.) *Managing Public Organizations: Lessons from contemporary European experience* (Sage, 1993)

Peters G., The Changing Nature of Public Administration: From Easy Answers to Hard Questions (2003) 5 *Viešoji Politika Ir Administravimas*

Pidd M., *Measuring the Performance of Public Services: Principles and Practice* (Cambridge University Press, 2012)

Prosser W., Privacy (1960) 48 *California Law Review*

Punch Newspaper (August 11, 2018)

Quah J., Ensuring Good Governance in Singapore: Is This Experience Transferable to Other Asian Countries? (2013) 26 (5) *International Journal of Public Sector Management*

Quelen R., Building Pro-Change Multisectoral Coalitions to Overcome the Resistance of Powerful Vested Interests' in Sina Odugbemi & Thomas Jacobson (eds.), *Governance Reform Under Real-World Conditions: Citizens, Stakeholder & Voice* (World Bank, 2008) http://siteresources. worldbank.org/EXTGOVACC/Resources/GovReform_ebook.pdf accessed 10ᵗʰ July 2018

Rao S., *Civil Service Reform: Topic Guide* (GSDRC, 2013) http://www.gsdrc. org/docs/open/csr_topicguide_2013.pdf accessed 12ᵗʰ April 2018

Reich C., The New Property (1964) 73 (5) *The Yale Law Journal*

Renn O., Webler T. & Wiedmann P., *Fairness and Competence in Citizens Participations: Evaluating Models for Environmental Disclosure* (Kluwer Academic 1995)

Right2Info, *Nigeria: The Limits to the Freedom of Information Act* (2011) http://www.right2info.org/recent/nigeria-the-limits-of-freedom-of-infor mation-act accessed 13ᵗʰ July 2015

Robert N., Direct Citizen Participation in Roberts N. C. (ed.) *The Age of Direct Citizens Participation* (Sharpe, 2008)

Robinson M., *From Old Public Administration to the New Public Service: Implications for Public Sector Reform in Developing Countries* (UNDP-Global Centre for Public Service Excellence, 2015) http://www.undp. org/content/dam/undp/library/capacity-development/English/Singapore %20Centre/PS-Reform_Paper.pdf accessed 9ᵗʰ March 2018

Rokkan S., Dimensions of State Formation and Nation-Building: A Possible Paradigm for Research on Variations within Europe, in C. Tilly, (ed.), *The Formation of National States in Western Europe* (Princeton University Press, 1975)

Rubakula G., The New Public Management and its Challenges in Africa (2014)

4 (4) *JJSTE* 86

Russell D., *The Role of the Executive Government in Australia* (Papers on Parliament No. 41, 2003)

Salminen A., New Public Management and Finnish Public Sector in Alberto Amaral, V. Lynn Meek (eds.) *The Higher Education Managerial Revolution?* (Kluwer Academic Publishers, 2003)

Savage A., Leaks, *Whistleblowing and the Public Interest: The Law of Unauthorised Disclosures* (Edward Elgar Publishing Ltd, 2016)

Schiavo-Campo S. & Sundaram P., Government Employment and Compensation—Facts and Policies in Schiavo-Campo S. & Sundaram P. (eds) *To Serve and To Preserve: Improving public administration in a competitive world* (Asian Development Bank, 2000) http://www.adb.org/sites/default/files/improving-public-administration.pdf accessed 27th March 2018

Selznick P., *Leadership in Administration: A Sociological Interpretation.* (University of California Press, 1984)

Sherman C., Law and Development Today: The New Developmentalism (2009) 9 (10) *German Law Journal*

Simone B. & Fritz V., *Making Public Sector Reforms Work: Political and Economic Contexts, Incentives & Strategies.* (Policy Research Working Paper 6174, World Bank 2012) http://siteresources.worldbank.org/EXT-PUBSECREF/Resources/civil_service_thematic_paper.pdf accessed 27th March 2018

Skidmore P., Bound K. & Lownsbrough H., *Community Participation: Who Benefits* (Joseph Rowntree Foundation, 2006) http://www.jrf.org.uk/system/files/1802-community-network-governance.pdf accessed 19th May 2016

State Service Commission, *Governance of Crown Entities* http://www.ssc.govt.nz/crown-entity-governance accessed 24th September 2017

Stillman R., *Public Administration: Concepts and Cases* (7th ed. Houghton Mifflin Company, 2000)

Suleiman A. & Oladimeji L., Public-Private Partnership and Infrastructural

Development in Nigeria: The Rail Transportation Sector in Focus (2015) 7 (4) *British Journal of Education, Society & Behavioural Science*

Syvertsen T., The Many Uses of the 'Public Service' Concept (1999) 20 *Nordicom Review* https://pdfs.semanticscholar.org/0919/8c809843e-25b4850368aa9174723cbf433af.pdf accessed 26th March 2018

Thoenig J., Institutional theories and public institutions: Traditions and appropriateness' in Peters Guy and Jon Pierre (eds), *Handbook of Public Administration* (SAGE, 2003) https://hal.archives-ouvertes.fr/halshs-00139954/document accessed 4th July 2016

Trubek D. & Santos A., Introduction: The Third Moment in Law and Development Theory and Emergence of a New Critical Practice' in D.M. Trubek and A. Santos (eds.), *The New Law and Economic Development: A Critical Appraisal* (Cambridge University Press, 2006)

Trubeck D., *Law and Development in the Twenty-first Century* (Law and the New Developmental State (LANDS) Research Papers, 2009)http://www.law.wisc.edu/gls/lands.html accessed 4th June 2018

UNDP- GPCSE, *From Old Public Administration to the New Public Service: Implications for Public Sector Reform in Developing Countries* (2016) http://www.undp.org/content/dam/undp/library/capacitydevelopment/English/Singapore%20Centre/PS-Reform_Paper.pdf accessed 9th May 2018

University of York, *Public Interest Test Method Statement* https://www.york.ac.uk/records-management/foi/foi-policy/public-interest-test-method-st atement/ accessed 30th August 2017

UN Public Administration Program, *The Role of Active Participation and Citizen Engagement in Good Governance* (2013) http://www.un.org/esa/socdev/egms/docs/2013/EmpowermentPolicies/Elia%20Armstrong%20presentation.pdf accessed 31st July 2018

Visionscape, *Private Sector Plan N50bl Corporate Green Bond To Finance #Cleanerlagosinitiative* https://www.visionscape-sanitation.com/private-sector-plan-n50bl-corporate-green-bond-to-finance-cleanerlagosinitiati ve/ accessed 11th July 2018

Walle S. & Scott Z., *The Role of Public Services in State and Nation-Building:*

Exploring Lessons from European History for Fragile States (GSDRC Research Paper, 2009) www.gsdrc.org/docs/open/con68.pdf accessed 3rd April 2018.

Weiss J., *Business Ethics: A Stakeholder's Approach & Issues Management Approach* (5th edn, South Western 2009)

Williams R., *Understanding Governance: Policy Networks, Governance, Reflexivity and Accountability* (Open University Press, 1997)

World Bank, *Republic of India: Corporate Governance of Central Republic Sector Enterprises* (June 2010) http://siteresources.worldbank.org/FI-NANCIALSECTOR/Resources/India_CG_Public_Sector_Enterprises.pdf accessed 13th April 2014

World Bank, *Government Support in Financing PPPs* https://ppp.worldbank.org/public-private-partnership/financing/government-support-subsidies accessed 12th July 2018

World Bank, *The World Bank Approach to Public Sector Management 2011-2020: Better Results from Public Sector Institutions* http://siteresources.worldbank.org/PUBLICSECTORANDGOVERNANCE/Resources/285741-1287520109339/PSM-Approach.pdf accessed 4th of July 2016

World Bank Group, *CPIA Africa: Assessing Africa's Policies and Institutions* (2017) http://documents.worldbank.org/curated/en/891501500349324004/pdf/117514-REVISED-96p-WB-CPIA-Report-July2017-ENG-v16.pdf accessed 21st March 2018

World Bank Group, *Law and Development Movement* http://siteresources.worldbank.org/INTLAWJUSTINST/Resources/LawandDevelopmentMovement.pdf accessed 4th June 2018

Worthington S., Reforming Director's Duties (2001) 64 (3) *Modern Law Review*

Weber E., *Peasants into Frenchmen: The Modernization of Rural France 1870–1914.* Stanford (Stanford University Press, 1976)

Electronic Sources

http://thelawdictionary.org/public-institution/ accessed 4th July 2016

http://www.fedcivilservice.gov.ng/?page_id=284 accessed 16th April 2018

http://www.ohcsf.gov.ng/index.php/scheme-of-service accessed 18th April 2018

http://lawnigeria.com/LawsoftheFederation/CODE-OF-CONDUCT-BUREA
U-ANDTRIBUNAL-ACT.html accessed 18th April 2018

http://www.oecd.org/dataoecd accessed 10th April 2016

http://www.pogoarchives.org/m/cots/Lloyd-LaFollette-Act.pdf accessed 10th
April 2018

https://rsbopp.rv.gov.ng/index.php/legislations/law accessed 22nd May, 2018

https://rsbopp.rv.gov.ng/index.php/about-us/mandate accessed 22nd May 2018

https://rsbopp.rv.gov.ng/index.php/legislations/law accessed 22nd May 2018

http://www.cleanerlagos.org/ accessed 4th July 2018

https://efccnigeria.org/ accessed 23rd May 2018

http://icpc.gov.ng/ accessed 23rd May 2018

http://csnacng.org/demand-for-the-investigation-of-the-ownership-of-vision
scape-sanitation-solutions-and-its-contract-with-the-lagos-state-govern
ment/ accessed 20th August 2018

https://efccnigeria.org/efcc/news/2681-efcc-to-appeal-acquittal-of-ex-adama
wa-gov-ngilari accessed 8th August 2018

http://edojudiciary.gov.ng/wp-content/uploads/2016/10/Federal-High-Court
-Civil-ProcedureRule.pdf accessed 23rd July 2019

www.ingramcontent.com/pod-product-compliance
Lightning Source LLC
Chambersburg PA
CBHW072106040426
42334CB00042B/2509